Merry Christmas Jeff!

Love, Terry, Peggy, Ryan, Morgan, Bryce & Bailey

Game of My Life

20 Stories of
Buffalo Bills Football

SAL MAIORANA

www.SportsPublishingLLC.com

ISBN: 1-58261-963-8

© 2005 by Sal Maiorana

Publishers: Peter L. Bannon and Joseph J. Bannon Sr.
Senior managing editor: Susan M. Moyer
Acquisitions editor: Bob Snodgrass
Developmental editor: Travis W. Moran
Art director: K. Jeffrey Higgerson
Dust jacket design: Heidi Norsen
Project manager: Jim Henehan
Imaging: Heidi Norsen
Photo editor: Erin Linden-Levy
Vice president of sales and marketing: Kevin King
Media and promotions managers: Mike Hagan (regional),
     Randy Fouts (national), Maurey Williamson (print)

Printed in the United States of America

Sports Publishing L.L.C.
804 North Neil Street
Champaign, IL 61820

Phone: 1-877-424-2665
Fax: 217-363-2073
Web site: www.SportsPublishingLLC.com

The game of my life is the game of life, and as I traverse through that life, I do so with the greatest team of all time—my family.

Thank you to my wife, Christine, my daughters, Taylor and Caroline, and my son, Holden, for providing your unending love and support.

CONTENTS

FOREWORD

By Steve Tasker

It seems today in America that everybody participates in sports, and usually not just one sport. At some time in their life, they have competed at some level, be it in a youth league, on a high school or college team, in an adult recreation league, or for the fortunate few—as a professional.

There are team sports and individual sports, something that fits everyone's taste or particular athletic skill, and regardless of what endeavor it may be, I would bet that everyone has a game, or a single moment that stands alone as their crowning achievement.

The stories that you will read in the pages that follow are the moments or performances of a group of athletes who reached the highest level of their chosen sport—the great sport of football—and they all did so while playing for the Buffalo Bills.

Most readers will be able to relate to the memories of these athletes because the same emotions are within all of us. What's important to one person is just as important to another whether it occurs on a national stage or not. Jim Kelly's six-touchdown game against the team he rooted for as a kid, the Pittsburgh Steelers, stands at the top for him, but it really is no different than the sense of pride and accomplishment that would be felt by a high school basketball player who may have scored the winning basket in the final seconds against the arch rival.

For me, the fun part about Sal Maiorana's *Game of My Life* is not the wins and losses recounted in each story, but the personal value that each person placed on each event. In that sense each of us is a part of every story. Bills fans will learn what it meant to Andre Reed to catch 15 passes in one game, what it meant to Reggie McKenzie and Joe DeLamielleure to block for O.J. Simpson, what it meant to Don Beebe to catch his first touchdown pass, and what it meant to Frank Reich to engineer the greatest comeback in NFL history.

You'll come to understand just how important these games were to those players you've watched through the years.

Remember that some of these stories are decades old, but believe me, for the men who are sharing these memories, they are timeless. Even as I recounted my own story of Super Bowl XXV, the emotions I felt at the time of that game were still bubbling close to the surface 14 years later. These men relive these moments not only to "relive the old magic" but to illustrate to the readers that when they say "Game of My Life," they mean it.

Some of these games defined players' careers, others marked great individual achievements, and some, in rare instances, were life changing. I am certain you will enjoy these stories from the past. The great players who share them have reason to be proud, not only because of the level of their achievement, but because they have forever etched their name into the rich history of the Buffalo Bills franchise.

ACKNOWLEDGMENTS

Every time I take on a book project, I save my most important 'thank you' on the Acknowledgment page—the one to my family—for the end. Therefore, here's a break in tradition.

Foremost, and this time first, I would like to thank the four people who mean more to me than anything—my wife, Christine, our son, Holden, and our daughters, Taylor and Caroline. I know if I asked Frank Reich what his greatest accomplishment was, he wouldn't tell me it was quarterbacking the Bills to the greatest comeback in NFL history—it would be his loving marriage and the children that union has produced. Writing a book (or in my case, 11 and counting) is an exhilarating achievement to be sure, but no more fulfilling than coming home every day and finding those four people waiting for me at the door.

I would like to thank the Bills' organization for their help in procuring photographs and research material, and in particular, here's a big shout out to Denny Lynch, the Bills' director of archives. Denny is a great friend who shares my passion for the history of the Bills and understands the importance of never forgetting the men of yesteryear who served the franchise. Thanks for all your help, as usual.

I would like to thank the many sports writers whose prose I used to conduct research for this project, most notably my comrades at the Rochester *Democrat and Chronicle*, Leo Roth and Scott Pitoniak, and my friends who work, or have worked for, the *Buffalo News*: Vic Carucci, Larry Felser, Milt Northrop, Mark Gaughan, Allen Wilson, Bucky Gleason, Bob DiCesare and Jerry Sullivan.

Thank you to photographer Robert L. Smith for contributing photographs. No one has taken more pictures of the Bills than Bob, and he has always been gracious in allowing me to use his photos to illustrate my Bills books. Also, to Mary Karen Delmont, archivist at my alma mater, Buffalo State College, who allowed me to pore through the old Buffalo *Courier-Express* photo files for additional pictures.

To the folks at Sports Publishing Inc. who do a great job churning out sports books and have hit a home run with their *Game of My Life* series of which I am thrilled to be a part. Thanks to Bob Snodgrass for signing me up, and to Travis Moran for editing me. It was a pleasure working with you, and I hope we can do it again.

Finally, thanks to all the players—and that one very special coach—who are featured in the following pages. They provided their time, their memories, and their insight, and if I did my job, I think you will find their stories to be interesting, entertaining, and truly memorable.

INTRODUCTION

I will never forget how sick I felt that night in Tampa, Florida. So, to some degree, I can imagine what it must have been like for the Bills in the moments after Scott Norwood's field goal attempt sailed wide right, preventing Buffalo from winning Super Bowl XXV.

As I sat up in the press box high above Tampa Stadium, the deadline for writing the most important story to that point in my newspaper career about 90 minutes away, I couldn't bring myself to start tapping away at the computer keys. It was the only time that has ever happened to me.

Oh, there have been times when I've stared blankly at the screen, unable to string cogent thoughts together, but this was the first time—and hopefully the last—that I simply didn't *feel* like writing.

When the officials standing under the goalposts signaled that Norwood's kick had missed, I felt like I had just been punched in the stomach. My brain went to sleep and as I watched in bitter disappointment as the New York Giants carried the Tuna—Bill Parcells—off the field in celebration, it occurred to me that there was no way I could write this story. It was just too depressing.

Fortunately, professionalism got the best of me and I managed to produce about a thousand semi-intelligent words, enough to fill the editorial hole that had been designated for me by my editors at the Rochester *Democrat and Chronicle*.

A native of Buffalo, I had grown up a Bills fan, and having followed the team for about two decades before trading in my aluminum seat out in Rich Stadium for one on press row, there was no game I wanted the Bills to win more than Super Bowl XXV.

And they should have won it. Norwood, a usually reliable placekicker, looked confident from what I could see when they showed his face on the television monitor just before he attempted the first and still only win-or-else field goal in Super Bowl history. There was no breeze to speak of in the stadium. It was a grass field that was always a little tougher to kick on, but it had held up well throughout the game. And while 47 yards was not a gimme, it wasn't out of Norwood's range.

Besides, fate and karma and God had to be on the Bills' side, right? And if not the Bills themselves, then certainly the team's loyal and long-suffering fans—the folks who sat through 20 straight losses to the Dolphins in the 1970s, through the back-to-back 2-14 seasons in the mid-1980s. They deserved to be Super Bowl champions. There's no way he can miss this kick, I thought, as he lined it up with more than 73,000 fans looking on breathlessly in the stadium and hundreds of millions of others around the world doing the same in front of their televisions.

Wide right?

It is the defining moment in the life of the Bills, and no Bills fan will ever forget it. But I found it interesting that when Steve Tasker, for this book, chose that game as the game of his life, he focused not on the missed field goal, nor the disappointment of the defeat, but on the circumstances and the emotion that surrounded that magnificent game.

He admitted that it was the only game in his career where he walked off the field feeling physically sick to his stomach, which was comforting for me to learn. But the memories he has of that day are of Whitney Houston singing the national anthem, of thousands of American flags being waved in the stands, of Apache helicopters hovering over the stadium, and the role the Bills and Giants were playing as they provided a three-hour respite for Americans troubled by the start of the Gulf War.

Tasker called it an "unforgettable day." And there have been dozens of unforgettable days in Bills history, 20 of which you will read about in the ensuing pages.

Some of the games are instantly recognizable. Can you guess what game Frank Reich picked? Naturally, the miraculous comeback victory over Houston in the 1992 playoffs. Reggie McKenzie chose the afternoon at Shea Stadium when he and the rest of the Electric Company helped O.J. Simpson become the first player in NFL history to surpass the 2,000-yard plateau. Joe Ferguson picked his greatest day as a professional when he threw for 419 yards as the Bills ended a 16-game Orange Bowl losing streak in Miami. And Fred Smerlas chose the game against the Jets when his blocked field goal at the end of regulation helped the Bills end years of misery as they clinched the AFC East division title and Fandemonium broke out at Rich Stadium.

Other games are not as recognizable. Hall of Famer Billy Shaw surprised me when he chose one of Buffalo's greatest disappointments, the loss in the 1966 AFL Championship Game that cost the Bills the opportunity to play in the first Super Bowl. Andre Reed chose a game in 1994, the year the Bills' run of six straight playoff years ended, but during that season he caught a Buffalo-record 15 passes against the Packers. And Cornelius Bennett picked a game he didn't even start. It was his first NFL appearance midway through the 1987 season after the Bills had acquired him in a blockbuster trade, and though he hardly knew what he was doing in the Buffalo defense, he created daylong havoc for John Elway and the Denver Broncos.

It was obvious to me in interviewing these men that the memories they have are memories they cherish. And their memories are, in most cases, the memories that we cherish as fans and reporters. I got the sense that they enjoyed reliving these memorable days in their careers, and I hope you enjoy reliving what are surely some of your memorable days.

CHAPTER ONE

Booker Edgerson

Position: Cornerback
Number: 24
Years with Bills: 1962-69
Other teams: Broncos (1970)
College: Western Illinois
Born: July 5, 1939
Birthplace: Baxter, Arkansas
Current residence: Buffalo, New York
Current occupation: Director of Equity and Diversity—Erie Community College.

Edgerson is a member of the Greater Buffalo Sports Hall of Fame…is a member of the Western Illinois Hall of Fame…was not drafted by an AFL or NFL team and signed as a free agent with the Bills…finished his Buffalo career with 23 interceptions in eight seasons…was traded to Denver in 1970 where ex-Bills coach Lou Saban was in charge, but his career ended halfway through the year because of a knee injury…won the 1993 Ralph C. Wilson Jr. Award…one of the most active members of Bills Alumni club.

THIS IS BOOKER EDGERSON

One way or another Booker Edgerson was destined to begin his pro football career under Lou Saban—the same coach who had recruited him to play for Western Illinois University and coached him his first two years at the school.

After guiding the Leathernecks to an undefeated record in 1959, Saban was offered a chance to jump into the pro ranks as head coach of the Boston Patriots in the fledgling American Football League. In February of 1960, he took the job, and three of his ex-players—Edgerson, Larry Garrett, and Leroy Jackson—told Saban: "Don't forget us when we graduate."

Saban didn't forget Edgerson, a speedy, athletic cornerback who excelled in man-to-man coverage.

"I was playing college baseball at the time, and I signed a contract with the Patriots, but in those days you couldn't participate in college sports and sign a professional contract," Edgerson recalled. "I just told them to hold on to it until the baseball season was over with."

By the time Edgerson was eligible to be signed in the 1962 draft—which was held in December of 1961—Saban was no longer associated with the Patriots. "He got fired so he asked me what I wanted to do with the contract," Edgerson said. "I said, 'Just tear it up and wherever you end up, give me a call.' I made an assumption he was going to end up somewhere in football."

Saban did end up somewhere: Buffalo, as the Bills' player personnel director. However, when draft day rolled around Saban must not have been able to convince the Bills' braintrust of general manager Dick Gallagher, head coach Buster Ramsey, and chief scout Harvey Johnson that Edgerson was a worthy selection. The Bills had 34 picks in that draft and not one was used on Edgerson.

Then again, no other professional team in the AFL or the NFL bothered to call Edgerson's name, so the five foot 10, 181-pounder who could run the 100-yard dash in 9.7 seconds was cast into football's version of purgatory: the free agent market.

About a month later, just when Edgerson was beginning to wonder what he was going to do with the rest of his life, his fortunes changed. At the conclusion of the 1961 season, Bills owner Ralph Wilson fired Ramsey and promoted Saban to be his replacement. Now with some power at his disposal, Saban told Wilson about this kid from Western Illinois who might be worth a shot as a free agent.

"Lou ended up in Buffalo, and he gave me a call," Edgerson recalled. "I said, 'Well, send me a contract.'"

Edgerson reported to training camp in the summer of 1962 and despite his past association with Saban, he was a long shot to make the roster. His

Booker Edgerson came to the Bills as an undrafted free agent out of Western Illinois University in 1962. **Courtesy of the Buffalo Bills**

college days were over—this was pro football, and there were no free rides. Edgerson had to earn his spot, and it was a laborious process because of his undrafted status.

"I was a little disappointed that I didn't start off being a starter, but they'd drafted a kid out of North Carolina [Tom Dellinger] so they wanted to take a look at him and a few other people," said Edgerson.

Each day Edgerson did all he could to persuade Saban and catch defensive coach Joe Collier's attention. Within a month, the coaches realized Edgerson was the best they had. On opening day, he was the starter at left cornerback—a position he would hold for the next eight years.

In his first professional game, Edgerson picked off two George Blanda passes during a 28-23 loss to the Oilers. He finished that season with six interceptions for 111 return yards and a spot on the AFL's All-Rookie team.

One of the reasons why Butch Byrd is the Bills' all-time leader in interceptions with 40, and not Edgerson: Teams were wary of throwing Edgerson's way so they often picked on Byrd, a physical, gambling player who sometimes could be burned by being too aggressive.

"Booker had a lot to do with my interception record," Byrd said. "Joe Collier, who was the defensive coach taught me the strategy, taught all of us the strategy on how to play defense but the game preparation and how to really play cornerback was Booker Edgerson."

GAME DAY SETTING

Houston was the dominant team in the AFL during the league's infancy as it won the first two championships in 1960 and 1961 behind a dynamic offense led by rejuvenated NFL castoff George Blanda.

Blanda had spent 10 years in the NFL with George Halas's Chicago Bears serving primarily as a backup quarterback, frustrated that he had rarely been given an opportunity to thrive as the starter. Disenchanted with football, he retired in 1958 and was content to move on with his life, but the birth of the AFL was a re-birth of sorts for him.

He joined the Oilers and in his first two seasons he threw 60 touchdown passes, including 36 in 1961—a record that was never broken in the decade that the league flew its own banner before the 1970 merger with the NFL.

The Oilers also reached the AFL Championship Game in 1962, losing to cross-state rival Dallas, but in the final seven years of the AFL, Houston managed only one more winning record. Just as the Oilers were beginning their descent, the Bills were climbing to position themselves to become the torchbearer of the AFL.

Buffalo won its first nine games in 1964 on the way to capturing the first of its two AFL championships. Two of those victories came against

This interception against Denver was one of 23 Edgerson made for the Bills during his eight-year career in Buffalo. **Courtesy of Buffalo Courier-Express**

Blanda's Oilers, a 48-17 shellacking in Houston and a 24-10 victory at the Rockpile in downtown Buffalo.

In the first meeting, the stout Buffalo defense held the potent Houston offense to eight first downs and 137 net yards and Oilers coach Sammy Baugh had benched Blanda in favor of young Don Trull.

When the Oilers arrived in Buffalo for the rematch, they were riding a four-game losing streak—longest to that point in franchise history—and Blanda was in an ornery mood. There was little question that spirals were going to be filling the crisp November air, especially after his last perform-ance against the Bills, so Edgerson and the Buffalo secondary were on alert.

THE GAME

Sunday, November 1, 1964
BILLS 24, OILERS 10

It was about an hour before the Bills and Oilers were going to battle at War Memorial Stadium, and Edgerson and Buffalo's star running back, Cookie Gilchrist, were nowhere to be found.

"That was the week Cookie and I got caught in the elevator at our apartment building," Edgerson remembered. "It was chaos. We went to breakfast and everything, and then we came back and were coming down the elevator and it got stuck. We got to the stadium right as the guys were going out for warmups."

Bills coach Lou Saban couldn't have been too pleased with the two players, but there wasn't much Saban could say afterward as Gilchrist rushed for 139 yards and a touchdown and Edgerson played what he calls the game of his life as the Bills stymied the Oilers, 24-10.

"What a day that was," Edgerson said. "First we had the problems before the game, and then George Blanda came out throwing the ball."

And he never stopped.

Blanda set pro football records for passes attempted (68) and passes completed (37), but it wasn't enough for the Oilers to overcome the talented Bills. Despite Blanda's 393 passing yards, Houston scored only 10 points against the rugged Buffalo defense as the Bills—dodging trouble all day—escaped with their eighth straight victory to start the 1964 season.

"He probably threw 20 to 25 passes my way, but at the end of the day it felt like he had thrown all 68 my way," said Edgerson. "Charley Hennigan was his best receiver and you throw to your best receiver. But the best thing for me is that even though he caught 12 passes (for 160 yards), he never scored."

Edgerson had a terrific game in 1968 against Joe Namath and the Jets at War Memorial Stadium, when he returned a "Broadway" Joe interception 45 yards for a touchdown.

"A lot of folks think the game with Namath when he threw five interceptions and I ran one back for a touchdown was my greatest game, but to me that Houston game was better," said Edgerson.

"Going against Charley Hennigan, who was one of the premier receivers at that time, and Blanda was in his prime doing a very good job. They completed a lot of passes, but they didn't score and we won the game."

In Buffalo's earlier victory at Houston, the Oilers' running game was nonexistent as Sid Blanks and Charlie Tolar were held to a combined 46 yards. Not that this was a shocking development. In 14 games that year the

Bills allowed their opponents just 913 rushing yards, a team record low that still stands more than four decades later, including the strike season of 1982 when the Bills played only nine games. Oilers coach Sammy Baugh recognized that running against the Bills was a lost cause, so he had Blanda attack through the air.

It looked to be a prudent strategy early on as Blanda twice drove the Oilers deep into Buffalo territory, and while Blanda missed a field goal to spoil the first possession he hit Willard Dewveall with an 11-yard touchdown pass on the second for a 7-0 lead.

Bobby Smith answered for Buffalo with a 37-yard touchdown run, but back came the Oilers as Ode Burrell returned the ensuing kickoff to midfield and Blanda kicked a 49-yard field goal for a 10-7 lead. Edgerson prevented a first down when he broke up a pass intended for Hennigan.

The Bills had given up 20 or more points just three times in their first seven games, and they had already allowed 10. Saban and Collier huddled the defense on the sideline and read it the riot act, but the Oilers continued to dominate the game on offense. However, while Blanda was ripping off chunks of yardage, he couldn't change the most important numbers: those on the scoreboard.

During the scoreless second and third quarters, Houston had four chances to extend its lead and failed every time. Safety George Saimes came up with a fumble recovery and an interception, and Blanda missed two more field goals.

"When that guy [Blanda] is right, he's just too tough," Saban said after the game. "I'm sure glad we don't have to look at him again this season. We expected George would be doing a lot of throwing against us, but not that much. The difference was we got the big plays when we needed them and they didn't."

Case in point: During an 80-yard drive that bridged the third and fourth quarters, Elbert Dubenion made a clutch 15-yard reception on a third-and-10 play, and Ernie Warlick made a 21-yarder on a first-and-15. That set the stage for Smith's three-yard touchdown run with 12:23 left to play, putting the Bills ahead, 14-10.

And then, as Houston threatened to answer by driving to the Buffalo 26, Dewveall dropped a fourth-down pass at the goal line, prompting an irritated Blanda to slam his helmet to the ground in disgust.

Houston's suspect secondary had been lit up by Jack Kemp in the first game as he threw for a career-high 378 yards. This time the Oilers were determined to shut down the passing game, but their double-teaming tactics left them susceptible to the run and the Bills finally took advantage after the Dewveall drop.

On a first-down play Gilchrist slammed through the line, broke a tackle, and burst through the secondary for a 60-yard touchdown run that extended Buffalo's lead to 21-10.

Now it was left for Edgerson to put the capper on the day. Another promising Houston drive advanced deep into Buffalo territory, but when Blanda tried to hit Hennigan on the sideline, Edgerson stepped in front, picked off the pass at the 1 and took off the other way, going 91 yards before he was hauled down by Blanks.

"When I intercepted the ball I ran it back as best as I could," said Edgerson. "I guess that everybody was in pursuit because I went from one side of the field halfway to the other side, back and forth. And finally, Sid Blanks stepped on my heel and I went down. Everybody said I just pooped out. I said, 'No, no, no, no. If you really look at the film close enough, you'll see that he stepped on the heel.' But nobody ever accepted that excuse. I was laying on the field and Blanks was laying on the sideline and Saban said, 'Well, we have to get you in condition.' I rose up and looked over to the sideline and that's when I saw Blanks. I said, 'What the hell? If he's tired, what makes you think I wouldn't be tired?' He's an offensive player. Offensive players are supposed to be in better shape than defensive players."

Not making it all the way to the end zone was further exacerbated by the fact that the Bills' offense failed to punch it in from the nine and had to settle for a Pete Gogolak field goal.

"I told Lou Saban, 'I got the ball all the way down to the nine and you guys couldn't even score,'" Edgerson said. "'You couldn't even get nine yards? You had to kick a field goal. So don't be telling me why I didn't score the touchdown. Why didn't they score the touchdown? They came in fresh.'"

SINCE THE GAME

Edgerson played eight years in Buffalo, then was traded to Denver in 1970 where Saban had moved on to become head coach, but a knee injury ended his season at the mid-point. He retired and returned to start his second life in Buffalo in the human resources field.

"To me, football was just something to do until I got out there [in the real world]," said Edgerson. "I knew eventually I was going to be out there working eight hours a day doing something."

He worked for New York Telephone and was an administrator in the now defunct Comprehensive Employment Training Act program in Erie County. In 1982, he went to work for Erie Community College where he remains today as the Director of Equity and Diversity.

"The jobs I've had all have been dealing with people," he said. "I always thought I was very people-oriented."

CHAPTER TWO

Jack Kemp

Position: Quarterback
Number: 15
Years with Bills: 1962-69
Other teams: Steelers (1957), Chargers (1960-62)
College: Occidental
Born: July 13, 1935
Birthplace: Los Angeles, California
Current residence: Bethesda, Maryland
Current occupation: Board of Directors—Empower America

Jack played in five AFL championship games, winning two, both with the Bills in 1964 and '65…was the AFL's MVP in 1965…is the AFL's all-time leader in passes attempted (3,055), completions (1,428) and yards passing (21,130)…co-founded the AFL Players' Association and was elected its president five times…was one of only 20 players who were in the AFL for its entire 10-year existence, and is a member of the AFL Hall of Fame…was inducted into the Bills' Wall of Fame in 1984 and into the Buffalo Sports Hall of Fame in 1992.

THIS IS JACK KEMP

You wouldn't know it on some days at War Memorial Stadium when beer cans and curse words came flying out of the stands and fans threatened to strap cement shoes to Jack Kemp's feet and throw him in the Niagara River.

But while Kemp may not have always been appreciated, there is no denying he was one of the finest players in Bills history—in fact, American Football League history—and the man most responsible for giving the city its first real dose of athletic credibility and respectability.

Not a lot has changed in Buffalo through the decades in regard to the city's beloved football team: Play well and win and the fans will bathe you in adoration. Play lousy and lose, and boos will cascade down like the snow in January.

"Booing is part of the game," said Kemp, who certainly ought to know.

The fans boo today as the 21st century Bills continue to disappoint. They booed the four-time Super Bowl participant Bills of the early 1990s on

After two years of terrible play at the quarterback position, Jack Kemp joined the Bills. Buffalo promptly enjoyed five consecutive winning seasons, winning two AFL championships. **Courtesy of Buffalo Courier-Express**

the rare occasion when those teams had a bad day. And back in the 1960s, even when the Bills were playing in three straight AFL championship games and winning two, those leather-lunged denizens at the old Rockpile never hesitated spewing venom if they weren't getting their hard-earned money's worth.

Naturally, like every quarterback who has ever played in Buffalo or anywhere else, Kemp was the primary target of that invective. He was a hero on the days when the Bills won, a bum on the days when the guys in the other jerseys caught his passes and the Bills lost.

"Quarterbacks get booed because you're the focus of attention, good or bad," Kemp reasoned. "I teased Jim Kelly a few years ago. He was telling me he was getting booed and I said, 'You know, Kelly, you don't like to get booed, but you wouldn't believe how I used to get booed. I really got booed. They used to throw things at me and hurl insults and Coke cans and beer bottles, and that was just coming out of my home in Hamburg. You should have seen what they did to me down at the ballpark.'

"He laughed and I laughed, but I think anyone who plays pro sports, particularly quarterback who is at the epicenter of the team's failure or success, is going to get unduly praised when you win and unduly criticized when you lose. It made me try harder and it got my dander up."

Kemp was born and raised in Los Angeles and stayed home to attend Occidental College in the city. He lettered in three sports, but football was his passion and he was named All-Southern California Intercollegiate athletic conference his last two years before graduating with a degree in Physical Education.

With a strong arm as his primary asset he was selected in the 17th round of the 1957 NFL Draft by the Lions, but with Bobby Layne still running the show in Detroit, Kemp was cut before the end of training camp. He had brief stints with the Steelers and the Giants (and with Calgary of the Canadian Football League) before he finally established himself in the fledgling AFL.

Kemp signed with the Los Angeles Chargers in 1960, threw for 3,018 yards and 20 TDs and took his team to the AFL title game where it lost 24-10 to Houston. The following year the Chargers relocated to San Diego, won the Western Division again, and repeated as runner-up to Houston, losing 10-3 to the Oilers in the AFL's second championship game.

Though championship-starved, Kemp was otherwise perfectly happy in San Diego, only 90 miles away from his hometown, making a life for himself and his young family while playing the game he loved. And then his fortunes took a drastic turn, in the end a turn for the better, though it sure didn't seem that way at first.

With Kemp sidelined early in 1962 by a broken thumb, Chargers coach Sid Gillman tried to hide Kemp on the injured deferred list—exposing him to waivers—so that he could sign a backup quarterback to take Kemp's spot while he was out. But Gillman's ploy blew up in his face when the Bills claimed Kemp, and they were legally awarded his services for the sum of a $100 waiver fee. Kemp was forced to pack up his life and move 3,000 miles east to Buffalo. That's right, Buffalo—where it snows.

"He didn't want to come to Buffalo, that was the last place he wanted to be because he had been born and raised in California," said Bills owner Ralph Wilson.

But Kemp made the adjustment, helped turn the Bills into winners, and ultimately made friends in high places in Western New York who later helped him kick off a decorated post-football career in politics.

"It turned out to be a blessing in disguise," he said. "My wife told me that one door closes in your life and another one opens. The door to the Buffalo Bills and politics and Congress really opened up that day when I realized I was going to go to Buffalo to play for Lou Saban and play for Ralph Wilson's team."

The Bills ruled the league in 1964 and '65—Kemp earning Associated Press AFL player of the year honors that second season—and then won their third straight Eastern Division crown in '66 only to lose the championship game to Kansas City. That loss cost Buffalo an opportunity to play in Super Bowl I against NFL champion Green Bay and set in motion the eventual unraveling of the team.

The Bills sank to unexplored depths the last three years in the AFL, winning just nine of 42 games, though Kemp wasn't around to be booed in 1968 as he sat out the entire 1-12-1 season with a knee injury. He retired following the 1969 football campaign to begin a new campaign: Running for the 31st Congressional district seat in the House of Representatives, his constituency the people of Buffalo and Erie County, many of whom had mercilessly booed him during his days with the Bills.

"Getting Jack Kemp solved our quarterback problems," said Billy Shaw, Buffalo's left guard during that era and now a member of the Pro Football Hall of Fame. "But the greatest compliment I can give Jack is that he was instrumental in a lot of people becoming better people."

GAME DAY SETTING

Thirty-five years before the celebrated Rob Johnson-Doug Flutie quarterback controversy raged in Buffalo, Bills coach Lou Saban turned quarterback controversy into an art form by the way he ferreted out playing time between his two very capable quarterbacks, Kemp and Daryle Lamonica.

According to the depth chart, Kemp was the starter, Lamonica the reliever, though many Bills fans felt it should be the other way around. Sometimes so did Saban, and in the second-to-last game of the 1964 season, with the Buffalo offense in a funk and the AFL Eastern Division championship still undecided, Saban benched Kemp and turned to Lamonica to provide a spark.

Lamonica, who would later become known as the Mad Bomber after his 1967 trade to Oakland, directed a 30-19 victory over a hapless Broncos team in Denver, though he hadn't played a very efficient game. Kemp—one of Buffalo's veteran leaders—spent that day at Bears Stadium seething on the sideline, and then on the plane ride back to Buffalo, he sat down next to Saban and spoke his mind.

Kemp never minded the spirited competition he had with Lamonica because, as he has long maintained, first in his football career and now as a politician, "I think competitiveness brings out the best in everybody." But deep down he felt he was the best quarterback in Buffalo, the quarterback who gave the Bills the best chance to win the upcoming winner-take-all showdown with Boston.

"I told Saban if he wanted to win he had to play me," Kemp said of the game at Fenway Park that would determine who was going to face Western champ San Diego in the AFL championship game. "I don't know why I said it. It wasn't putting down Lamonica at all because he made me a better quarterback, but I told Saban, 'If you start me, I guarantee that I'll win this game for you.'"

Kemp always knew exactly what to say, and when to say it, and this was no exception. Saban had never wanted to win a game more than this one. Fired by the Patriots as their head coach midway through 1961, beating Boston had become an obsession with Saban. However, since taking over in Buffalo in 1962 his Bills had managed just one victory in six tries against the Patriots. Most recently, Boston had snapped the Bills' nine-game winning streak to start the 1964 season with a 36-28 triumph in Buffalo. That came on the heels of a 26-8 victory in Buffalo the previous December in a special playoff game to decide the 1963 division champion.

It didn't seem possible as the Bills were reeling off those nine straight wins that they would be in a must-win situation in Boston. But the Patriots had methodically churned through their schedule and thanks to that critical victory over the Bills a month earlier, the 10-2-1 Patriots were in position to win the division for a second straight year if they could continue their mastery of Buffalo.

And back in an era when players weren't afraid to say what they felt, the Patriots spent the week publicly exuding their confidence, predicting victory in the big game.

"Saban isn't saying who he'll start," Boston defensive end Larry Eisenhauer said. "But whether it's Lamonica or Kemp, it won't make a difference, we'll still beat 'em."

However, all the Patriots did was stoke the fire that was burning in the belly of every Bill, particularly Kemp, who wanted to prove once and for all that he was the No. 1 quarterback in Buffalo.

Jack Kemp ranks third behind Jim Kelly and Joe Ferguson in nearly every major Bills passing category. **Courtesy of Buffalo Courier-Express**

THE GAME

Sunday, December 20, 1964
BILLS 24, PATRIOTS 14

A few years after Kemp played the game of his life in helping the Bills roll past the Patriots—his football career done and his political career in full swing—he attended an election function where future Speaker of the House Tip O'Neill was the featured orator.

"Tip O'Neill was in the stands that day in Boston," Kemp said in reference to the staunch liberal Democrat from Massachusetts whose views were the polar opposite of Kemp's conservative Republican bent. "He was the majority leader at the time and he came up to Buffalo to make a speech and I was scared to death of what he might say. He came up and I was on the stage with my opponent and he introduced me and said 'Hey folks, you've got a tiger on the football field and a tiger in the Congress.' I think Tip O'Neill got me re-elected that year."

O'Neill was among the 38,021 frostbitten partisan Patriot patrons who braved a severe winter storm in hopes of watching their team lock up a second consecutive division title, only to file out cold, wet and disappointed after Kemp and the Bills throttled Boston.

"The snow was unbelievable, so they cleared off the field and we started about an hour late and then we just played one of the best games of our lives, even better than when we beat the Chargers in the two championship games," Kemp said in recalling Buffalo's dominating 24-14 victory.

More than a foot of snow fell on Boston the morning of the game and the Fenway Park grounds crew needed additional time to get the field in reasonable playing shape. Still, it was a mess, and Boston coach Mike Holovak opined that the poor conditions played in Buffalo's favor.

"I don't want to make excuses, but I think the weather hurt us and helped them," he said. "With two big backs like [Cookie] Gilchrist and [Wray] Carlton, they can move the ball a lot better on the ground. The footing was tough on our receivers and it took a lot out of our blitzing. But the Bills played well, they deserved it."

No one played better than Kemp. Yes, Holovak's point was well taken. The poor footing slowed Boston's defensive line and linebackers and Kemp had more time to pick out receivers who had an advantage over the defensive backs because they knew where they were cutting. But Kemp had to be sharp throwing a wet, frozen ball, and he was. He completed 12 of 24 passes for 286 yards and a touchdown, plus scored a pair of touchdowns on quarterback sneaks.

"I look back and people talk to me and say, 'Why wasn't Lamonica in?' and this and that," said guard Billy Shaw. "Well, I'm sorry, but when I was there, Jack Kemp was the quarterback. He was the man. He was the best we had at that particular time. Lamonica later went on and became a great football player, but I feel at that particular time Kemp was the man for us. Even though Daryle came in a few times and pulled a game out after a long pass for a touchdown, Jack was a great guy and a great leader who was smart."

Being a Southern Californian, Kemp did not have an affinity for snow, but he knew he could take advantage of the conditions with his bruising running backs, Gilchrist and Carlton, and speedy receivers Elbert Dubenion and Glenn Bass. At day's end, Dubenion had three catches for 127 yards, Bass six for 103.

"We didn't do anything new or unusual," said Kemp, who played an entire game for the first time since the season opener. "We knew the plays would go if we kept our mistakes to a minimum. I made a couple [three interceptions], but fortunately they didn't hurt us too much."

One of the keys for Buffalo was the play of its rugged offensive line. Led by Shaw, Stew Barber and Al Bemiller, the line protected Kemp from Boston's array of blitzers. "The big thing was the blocking," Kemp admitted. "Boston's blitzers were being picked up quickly and I had plenty of time for Dubenion and Bass to get down field."

Defensively, the Bills stuffed Boston's running game, limiting Larry Garron, Carl Garrett and company to just 33 yards, the seventh time the Bills allowed 52 yards or less in 1964. Boston quarterback Babe Parilli did throw for 294 yards, but his two touchdown passes to Tony Romeo simply weren't enough.

On the first play of the game, Carlton knew the Bills were in for a big day because Gilchrist was fired up.

"We got the ball on the first series of downs," Carlton remembered. "We had a play called 35 slide and Cookie ran the ball and picked up like eight, nine yards and just ran over the cornerback [Chuck Shonta]. Just knocked him cold, flattened him—first play of the game. And on the way back to the huddle, the Boston players are kind of standing around waiting for them to carry this guy off the field and Cookie pointed at them and said, 'Which one of you is next?' And I was kind of like, 'Whoa, we're in business.'"

Just 5:37 into the game, Kemp hit Dubenion with a 57-yard touchdown pass. Boston answered with a 72-yard touchdown drive as Romeo found a seam in the Buffalo defense and was all alone to haul in Parilli's 37-yard scoring pass, but the Bills maintained a 7-6 lead when Parilli's two-point conversion throw went awry when wide-open Gino Cappelletti fell on the slick turf.

Kemp's 52-yard bomb to Dubenion had the Bills knocking on the door late in the first quarter, but his first interception, by Ron Hall in the end zone, ruined that threat. Undaunted, the Buffalo defense forced a punt, and on the second play of the second quarter Kemp fired a 44-yard pass to tight end Ernie Warlick that carried to the Boston 10, and Kemp eventually scored on a third-down sneak to make it 14-6.

After the teams traded interceptions, Buffalo marched 65 yards to Pete Gogolak's 12-yard field goal 24 seconds before halftime, a 33-yard Kemp to Bass pass connection the key. "After we stung them with a couple of long ones, I knew we'd be in good shape," said Kemp.

Following a scoreless third quarter, Buffalo safety Charley Warner picked off a Parilli pass early in the fourth and returned it 38 yards to the Patriots 17. Carlton then broke a 14-yard run on third-and-nine to set up another Kemp touchdown sneak, and with a little more than 10 minutes to play, the Bills were firmly in command at 24-6.

Saban was beside himself with joy in the locker room. "This is the greatest victory I've ever had, especially after all the nonsense from this city," he said. "There will never be another victory like this for me. We've had to sit back and take a lot of stuff, but that's all immaterial. My everlasting thanks to you [the players] for beating Boston."

SINCE THE GAME

Six years after the game in snowy Boston, Kemp concluded that he'd had enough of football and moved into the political arena.

"I loved politics, but I never thought I would go into politics," Kemp said. "I was captain of the team and the president of the players' union; I was a clubhouse lawyer. I was always the guy who loved to organize and represent the players. And I loved giving speeches about free enterprise and America and patriotic messages. Finally, in 1969, the chairman of the Republican Party in Erie County said to me, 'Hey Kemp, if you ever want to run for Congress, I'd love to have you run as a Republican.'

"In 1970 after the AFL all-star game, my last game, I came home, talked to my wife, and said, 'I think I'm going to run for Congress.' I had a four-year no-cut contract with the Bills and I figured if I lost, I could come back and still play, either for Buffalo or maybe they'd trade me. I ran, I won and it's been downhill ever since."

He began as Representative of New York's 31st congressional district and spent nine terms in the House, including seven years as chairman of the powerful House Republican Leadership Conference. He ran for President in 1988, lost the nomination to George H. Bush, and served as Secretary of Housing and Urban Development in the Bush administration from 1989-92.

In 1996 he was Bob Dole's Vice Presidential running mate, losing to the Bill Clinton-Al Gore ticket, and since then Kemp has worked for Empower America, the free market Washington-based public policy and advocacy organization that he co-founded along with William Bennett, Jeanne Kirkpatrick, and Vin Weber.

"The thing that I admired most about Jack was the way that he handled himself," said Shaw. "He had political platforms that he certainly supported and we all knew where he stood, but he never tried to cram any of that down our throats. And there was no doubt in any of our minds, either during football or after football, that he would be on a political platform somewhere. I think our country missed the boat; if every voter knew him like I know him, then he would have been in a much higher office than he held."

CHAPTER THREE

Billy Shaw

Position: Offensive guard
Number: 66
Years with Bills: 1961-69
Other teams: None
College: Georgia Tech
Born: December 15, 1938
Birthplace: Natchez, Mississippi
Current residence: Toccoa, Georgia
Current occupation: Regional manager for concrete operations—Hughes Supply Company.

Billy played his entire nine-year career in the AFL and is a member of the AFL Hall of Fame...is the only player ever inducted into the Pro Football Hall of Fame (1999) without ever playing in the NFL...was a first-team All-AFL selection four times (1963-66) and second-team pick in 1968 and 1969...played in eight AFL all-star games and was named to the all-time AFL Team....made the pro football All-Decade team of the 1960s...is a member of the Georgia Tech Hall of Fame.

THIS IS BILLY SHAW

Tom Landry, the legendary coach of the Dallas Cowboys, recognized Billy Shaw as a player who possessed definite pro potential when he came out of Georgia Tech and entered the 1961 draft. Mind you, not as an offensive lineman where Shaw earned first-team All-SEC honors as a senior, but as a linebacker, a position he had never played in his life.

It was because of Landry's misguided evaluation of Shaw that the Buffalo Bills wound up procuring the services of a player who ultimately became one of the finest offensive linemen in the history of the game. In fact, in 1999 he became the only man in pro football history to earn induction into the Pro Football Hall of Fame without ever playing a down in the NFL, having played his entire nine-year career in the AFL with the Bills.

"I never played linebacker before and I just didn't want to try to play a new position," said Shaw, who was selected by Buffalo in the 1961 AFL draft which was conducted in late November 1960, then was picked by the Cowboys a month later in the NFL draft.

Upon choosing Shaw in the second round, No. 11 overall, the Bills' braintrust of general manager Dick Gallagher, coach Buster Ramsey, and chief talent scout Harvey Johnson assured Shaw he would play somewhere on the offensive line and perhaps a little at defensive end, another position he had played for the Yellow Jackets.

Shaw filed that information away, then waited to see what would happen when the NFL teams made their selections. Dallas, like Buffalo, had debuted as a franchise in 1960 and had just concluded its first NFL season. When the Cowboys waited until the 14th round to call Shaw's name, No. 184 overall, that got Shaw thinking that perhaps the established NFL didn't respect his talent and it might not be the best place for him. And then Landry revealed his plan for Shaw, and that made his decision quite simple.

"I signed with the Bills because they were going to play me at positions that I was used to playing," said Shaw.

And from 1961 through 1969, Shaw never stopped rewarding the Bills for the faith they showed in him. He anchored Buffalo's stout offensive line while playing his way into eight AFL all-star games and onto pro football's all-decade team of the 1960s. More importantly, he helped the Bills win three straight AFL East Division titles and two AFL championships.

Eddie Abramoski, who served as the Bills' head trainer for the first 35 years of their existence, has never forgotten the first time he saw Shaw.

"It was late in our first season [1960], and we had just drafted him and he came up to Buffalo for a visit," Abramoski said. "It was about 55 degrees in that old locker room [at War Memorial Stadium] and he had a topcoat on and his eyes were flitting around. He leans over to Harvey Johnson and

That Billy Shaw was a special player was obvious from the moment he was selected in the 1961 draft. The former Georgia Tech standout was inducted into the Pro Football Hall of Fame in 1991. **Courtesy of Robert L. Smith (Orchard Park, NY)**

says, 'Mr. Johnson, I don't know if I can play in this cold weather,' and I'm thinking, 'Billy, you don't know what cold weather is.'"

Abramoski recalls Johnson laughing at Shaw, a native of Mississippi who had always lived in the south, and reassuring him that he'd do "fine."

"Fine" would be an understatement.

"Of all the offensive linemen I played with in my 10 years, other than tackle Ron Mix [also a Hall of Famer], my old roommate with the Chargers, Billy Shaw is the greatest lineman in the history of the American Football League," said the man Shaw protected, quarterback Jack Kemp. "He ranked right there, parallel with Mix."

Shaw was the classic pulling guard of the 1960s, a time when athleticism was just as important for an offensive lineman as bulk and strength. Shaw played at about 260 pounds, but he could run like a back and he was strong as an ox. He could get out in front of a sweep and snowplow his way—in Buffalo, sometimes literally—through the defense. Or he could stand up in pass protection and hold off the biggest and the best of the AFL's sack artists, men like Ernie Ladd, Earl Faison, Bobby Bell, and Buck Buchanan.

Beyond his obvious physical skills and his undeniable accomplishments, what set Shaw apart from so many players was his demeanor and the kind of man he was. He was selected as the Bills' offensive captain in 1962, a 22-year-old kid playing in his second professional season. He never relinquished that role, even when a future politician and charismatic leader named Kemp joined the team.

"The reason Billy was the captain was every single person on the team respected the hell out of him," said Paul Maguire, then the Bills' punter who is now a television football analyst for ESPN. "He was such a great player. He was the kind of guy you can count on when you're playing. Players weren't electing him because he was the most popular guy."

Shaw was very much in the mold of Green Bay's Jerry Kramer who gained far more attention and fame because Kramer played in the NFL for Vince Lombardi's dynastic Packers. But Larry Felser, the former sports writer and columnist for the *Buffalo News* and a former Hall of Fame voter who was largely responsible for getting Shaw inducted into the shrine, has long maintained that "Any guy who knows football will tell you Shaw was a better player than Kramer."

One such guy was respected NFL personnel guru Ron Wolf who began his career in the '60s when Shaw was wreaking havoc on opposing defenses, and who, three decades later like Felser, helped convince voters of Shaw's Hall worthiness.

Wolf wrote in a letter to the voters that Shaw was one of the best two guards he'd ever seen play, and opinions on Shaw's candidacy began to change. When word came in January 1999—30 years after he retired—that his bust would forever be on display in Canton, Shaw felt a great sense of pride and joy, but perhaps more than anything, satisfaction.

"Waiting 30 years made it very, very special," Shaw said. "And to represent all of the guys who toiled in the AFL in obscurity for those many years makes it all much more special. If Ron Wolf walked through my door, I wouldn't know him because I don't think I ever met him, but it means a great deal to me to hear what he said."

Shaw is a regular visitor to Buffalo these days, always taking part in the team's alumni reunions and functions. He hasn't lived in Western New York for more than 35 years, but the area and its people continue to hold a special place in his heart.

"Buffalo was a great place to play," he said. "The people of Buffalo are wonderful, they took this southern boy in and put their arms around me. I can't say enough for the treatment I received from the people of Buffalo. I came to Buffalo when I was 21, just married, my first child was born there, and I left when I was 30. So up to that point I lived a third of my life in Buffalo and it was the most important time of my life. I couldn't imagine playing anywhere else. I couldn't imagine not being a Bill."

GAME DAY SETTING

Following Buffalo's 1965 championship, coach Lou Saban shocked his team and all of Buffalo by resigning to take the head coaching position at the University of Maryland, and defensive coordinator Joe Collier was promoted to replace him.

Through no fault of Collier's, it became clear in 1966 that the Bills were starting to lose their grip on league superiority. Age and some key injuries began to take their toll, the lack of team speed was a glaring problem, and the rise of teams such as Kansas City, Boston, Oakland and the Joe Namath-led New York Jets threatened Buffalo's reign.

However, this was still a gritty, veteran team that Collier inherited, and after a pair of startling blowout losses to the Chargers and Chiefs to open the season, the Bills regrouped for one last run at glory. They were 3-3-1 at the midway point of the schedule, but consecutive wins over the Jets, Miami, the Jets again, Houston and Oakland by a cumulative score of 149-56 thrust Buffalo back into the hunt for its third straight East Division crown.

The Bills traveled to Boston for a December showdown with the Patriots and they had a chance to clinch the division. Instead, their 14-3 loss put Boston into the driver's seat and when the Patriots blew out Houston the following week while Buffalo was idle, the Bills' chances for the division title seemed remote.

All Boston had to do was defeat Namath's Jets at Shea Stadium on the final Saturday, and that would render Buffalo's season finale on Sunday against Denver at the Rockpile meaningless. Bills's owner Ralph Wilson flew to New York to watch the Jets-Patriots game, and when it was over and Namath had thrown for 287 yards and three touchdowns in the Jets' surprising 38-28 victory, Wilson entered the New York locker room and asked, "You fellows want some champagne sent in here?"

Of course, the Bills still had to take care of their own business the next day, and with signs hung in the stadium proclaiming "Namath for President in '68" the Bills rolled over the hapless Broncos, 38-21, to win the division with a record of 9-4-1.

There was every reason for Collier to feel confident about Buffalo's chances against the Chiefs in the title game. After losing their home opener, 42-20, to Hank Stram's team, Buffalo had gone to Kansas City's Memorial Stadium and won 29-14. Quarterback Jack Kemp had a record of 7-1-1 against the Chiefs in his career as a Bill with 16 touchdown passes, and the Bills were hosting the game.

AFL followers knew in order for Buffalo to become the first team in AFL or NFL history to win three straight league titles, it would have to play a nearly perfect game against a Kansas City team led by the likes of Buck Buchanan, Bobby Bell, Len Dawson, Mike Garrett, Otis Taylor, Chris Burford, Willie Lanier, and Johnny Robinson.

"The Chiefs teams were probably the most physical we played," Shaw recalled. "Overall as a team, Kansas City had the most phenomenal athletes. They had a defense that was just unreal. They were the hardest team for us to match up with because I think they were physically that much stronger than us. They were superior to us in strength, and they were mobile."

The day before the game Collier was asked how many times he had seen the Chiefs play. "Well, I've seen them the two times we've played them and about six times on film. In fact, I'm sick of watching them."

Little did he realize how sick he would be on game day.

THE GAME

Sunday, January 1, 1967
CHIEFS 31, BILLS 7

It wouldn't become officially recognized as the Super Bowl game until Joe Namath's Jets stunned the world by defeating the Baltimore Colts in January 1969, but Shaw, his Bills teammates, and their opponents, the Kansas City Chiefs, knew what was at stake at War Memorial Stadium on New Year's Day 1967.

The winner of the 1966 AFL championship game would get to participate in the first pro football world championship game, carrying the banner of the rebellious AFL against the champions of the old, established NFL, the Green Bay Packers.

"Certainly it's hard to envision the magnitude of the Super Bowl as it exists today, but we knew that with the merger of the two leagues being inevitable, this was the first step," Shaw said. "That's why when you ask me what the game of my life was, even though it's a negative in that we lost the game, that's the one.

"I wanted to win that football game more than any football game I ever played. The '64 and '65 championship games were great highlights, but the one I remember the most was the one we lost to Kansas City. Being the first team from the AFL to play in the Super Bowl, it's one that people talk about and remember and it would have been wonderful to have played in it. We were so close, and if we had played Kansas City a decent game it would have been a different story, but we got mauled, we got killed. That one hurt."

The Bills had won the 1964 championship game over San Diego on their home field, but with a berth in the newfangled world championship game on the line, the '66 title game was regarded as the biggest sporting event to ever be held in Buffalo.

A sellout crowd of 42,080, largest ever to witness an AFL championship game, turned out on a raw winter day to watch the Bills go for the three-peat, and expectations were high that Buffalo would achieve history.

However, it was evident on the very first play that lady luck wasn't going to be shining on the Bills when Buffalo's Dudley Meredith fumbled the kickoff and Kansas City's Jerrel Wilson recovered at the 31. Three plays later Dawson, who in 1966 led the AFL in passing for the third time in five years and had thrown 26 TDs compared to just 10 interceptions, capitalized on the giveaway. He executed a flawless play-fake and when he looked up, the Buffalo defense had bitten and tight end Fred Arbanas was wide open to haul in a 29-yard touchdown pass.

"I remember we got off to a bad start," Shaw recalled.

And it never really got any better.

True, on the ensuing Buffalo possession the Bills answered the Kansas City touchdown as Jack Kemp beat a blitz and fired a 69-yard scoring pass to Elbert Dubenion who was all alone after cornerback Fred Williamson, playing one-on-one, slipped in the muck. "We could have used a few more plays like that," said Dubenion.

Thereafter the Chiefs simply stupefied the Bills on both sides of the ball. Offensively, Dawson pecked away at the Buffalo defense with short passes and running plays that weren't big yardage producers, but effectively milked the clock. Defensively, Kansas City's stout unit limited Buffalo to nine first downs, 40 harmless rushing yards and forced three turnovers.

Early in the second quarter Kansas City grabbed the game by the throat and didn't let go when Dawson whipped a 29-yard TD pass to Otis Taylor on a third-down play to make it 14-7.

The game's crucial moment occurred late in the half as the Bills drove toward a potential tying touchdown. From the 11-yard line Kemp tried to squeeze one in to Bobby Burnett at the goal line, but safety Johnny Robinson picked it off and raced 72 yards the other way, setting up a Mike Mercer field goal three seconds before halftime for a 17-7 lead.

"He made a great individual play," Kemp said of Robinson. "I thought we had him occupied, but he came in on a freelance to get between Bobby and the ball. I put everything I had on that pass, it was as hard as I can throw."

Although the third quarter was scoreless, the Chiefs maintained control as the Bills continued to stumble on offense.

"We put the pressure on our defense, and while we were a really good defensive team, the offense probably gave up 21 points that day," said Shaw. "We certainly didn't help them that day."

In the final period, Dawson's 45-yard pass to Chris Burford set up Mike Garrett's one-yard plunge into the end zone on a fourth and goal. And then the Buffalo offense provided one more gift a few minutes later when Kemp was sacked, lost the ball, and Bobby Hunt recovered for the Chiefs and returned it to the Bills' 21. Three plays later from the 18, Garrett scored the clinching touchdown on a dazzling reversal-of-field run.

"It's hard to remember the sequence of events, but I just know how frustrated we all felt because we were a better football team than we showed that day," said Shaw. "The fans in Buffalo had been so supportive through the years, and to let them down, I almost get emotional talking about it now and it happened how many years ago? To let them down, to let our families down, to let our teammates down. I remember that more than all the great wins and individual things that happened."

SINCE THE GAME

Buffalo News columnist Steve Weller opined following the loss to the Chiefs that "The AFL no longer belongs to Buffalo. The deed changed hands on New Year's Day."

"That was the passing of the torch," Shaw agreed. "It was Houston early, then San Diego, then we took the torch from San Diego in '64 and '65, and then Kansas City took it from us. They got beat in that first Super Bowl, but four years later they went and won the Super Bowl."

The Bills never challenged for an AFL championship in the final three years of the league's existence and Shaw's career was never the same. He suffered a knee injury in 1967 and missed a chunk of that disappointing 4-10 season. And then in 1968 and '69 he was bothered by nagging ailments that slowed him down, though Buffalo's disgraceful combined record of 5-22-1 those two seasons probably hurt more.

As the Bills were preparing to join the newly merged NFL in 1970, Shaw was calling it quits after playing in his final AFL all-star game. He'd had enough of football and decided to spend more time with his wife Patsy and their three daughters.

"It got to the point where football was abusing my family," Shaw said. "I promised myself and I promised my family that I would never let football abuse me, nor would I ever abuse football."

Shaw moved back down south and enjoys a successful business career. He founded his own pre-cast concrete company in Toccoa, Georgia which he ran almost continuously until he retired in 1994, a retirement that lasted about three months before he realized he needed activity in his life. Thus, he got back into the pre-cast concrete business, managing the southeast area for Hughes Supply of Orlando—a job he holds today.

CHAPTER FOUR

Ed Rutkowski

Position: Quarterback
Number: 40
Years with Bills: 1963-68
Other teams: None
College: Notre Dame
Born: March 21, 1941
Birthplace: Kingston, Pennsylvania
Current residence: Hamburg, New York
Current occupation: Western District Director for New York State's office
of Parks, Recreation, and Historic Preservation.

Ed was originally signed as a free agent out of Notre Dame to play in the defensive backfield, but later played as a wide receiver, quarterback, running back, kick and punt returner…upon retirement worked as Jack Kemp's administrative assistant the first eight years of Kemp's political career…later held office of Erie County Executive for eight years.

THIS IS ED RUTKOWSKI

In Buffalo, they used to call Ed Rutkowski the "Disaster Quarterback," but as Rutkowski likes to say, "The disaster happened before I went in, not after I went in."

That was certainly the case in 1968 when Rutkowski was one of five players who took snaps at quarterback, none of whom was longtime starter Jack Kemp, who missed the entire year with a knee injury, creating the free-for-all situation in the first place.

America didn't have a very good 1968, and neither did the Bills. U.S. troops were fully engaged in the Vietnam War and the nation was nastily divided on the issue of whether American soldiers should have been fighting at all in Southeast Asia. Protesters disrupted every conceivable type of event, from peace rallies to the Summer Olympics in Mexico City to the Democratic national convention in Chicago, and just about everything in between. Racial tensions boiled over, especially after the murder of civil rights leader Dr. Martin Luther King Jr. The presidential race was altered when leading Democratic candidate Robert Kennedy was gunned down two months after King, and that ultimately helped Republican Richard Nixon win the election.

And back in Buffalo, folks were eating La Nova pizza and drinking Utica Club beer, spending their hard-earned Bethlehem Steel checks at Sattlers, Twin Fair and Hengerer's, driving on the newly opened Kensington Expressway, summering at Crystal Beach, and lamenting their sad Bills as they hit rock bottom as a football franchise.

But 1968 wasn't so bad for Rutkowski, the handsome and popular Notre Dame alum who that year added another layer of duty to his already diverse role on the team when he stepped under center late in the season.

During his six years with Buffalo, Rutkowski was the guy every one of his coaches—Lou Saban, Joe Collier and Harvey Johnson—turned to when they needed something done. Need someone to play cornerback, running back, tight end, wide receiver, punt returner, kickoff returner and, yes, quarterback? Eddie was your guy, and he wasn't going to embarrass you or the team.

"I prided myself on playing a lot of positions well," said Rutkowski, the ultimate utility man whose breed no longer populates today's NFL. "I returned kicks, I kicked off a couple times, I made the team originally as a defensive cornerback if you can believe that. I played halfback, wide receiver, one game I played tight end for Ernie Warlick when he was hurt, and I played quarterback. If I was going to replace somebody as a starter, I wanted to play as well as, or better than, that individual. There aren't many guys who can say they played all those positions and played them fairly well. And I was cheap."

Ed Rutkowski was one of the most versatile players in Bills history. He played quarterback, running back, receiver, tight end, defensive back, and on special teams during his career. **Courtesy of the Buffalo Bills**

Rutkowski was born and raised in Kingston, Pennsylvania, a small town located in the northeast section of the state near Scranton and Wilkes-Barre. After a notable high school career, both academically and athletically, he enrolled at Notre Dame in the hope that he would play quarterback for the Irish. Another fella, a guy by the name of Daryle Lamonica, went to Notre Dame for the same reason.

"When I was in high school I was a heavily recruited quarterback and so was Daryle," Rutkowski remembered. "Every time I went someplace they said, 'You don't want to go to Notre Dame because there's a hotshot quarterback from California who's going to go there.' When we got out to Notre Dame, Daryle said the same thing was happening to him. People were saying, 'You don't want to go to Notre Dame, there's a hotshot quarterback from Pennsylvania who's going there.' We were kind of standoffish to each other when we first met, but then we became very close friends."

The hotshot from California beat out the hotshot from Pennsylvania, so the hotshot from Pennsylvania was switched to halfback and for three years took handoffs from the hotshot from California.

"Our sophomore year we had a series of injuries at halfback so they switched me from quarterback to halfback because I was the fastest quarterback," said Rutkowski. "To this day I always tell Daryle, 'If you were faster than me they would have switched you and I would have stayed at quarterback and made all the money you made.'"

While the three Notre Dame teams Lamonica quarterbacked in 1960, '61 and '62 achieved a lackluster 12-18 combined record, he enjoyed individual success as he tied an Irish record with four TD passes in a game against Pitt, then was named MVP of the 1962 East-West Shrine game when he threw for 349 yards. That prompted the Bills to select Lamonica in the 24th round of the 1963 draft.

Meanwhile, Rutkowski, who enjoyed more collegiate success on the track and the wrestling mat than he did on the football field, was ignored by every professional team in the AFL and NFL. He was all set to put his political science degree to use, but when Buffalo drafted Lamonica, Rutkowski and another Notre Dame grad, Ed Hoerster, decided to try to make the Bills as free agents.

"I never really planned on playing professional football," said Rutkowski. "The three of us were very good friends and we decided we'd just give it a shot and see what happened. And it so happened that Daryle and I made the team."

Right away coach Lou Saban recognized that Rutkowski was a man of many talents, but in a game against the offensively electric San Diego Chargers, Saban found out that cornerback might not be Rutkowski's best position. One of the starting corners, Booker Edgerson, was knocked woozy on a play and Rutkowski was sent in to replace him. When the Chargers broke their huddle, who came trotting out to Rutkowski's side? Future Hall of Famer Lance Alworth, who schooled the rookie with an out pattern that went for 15 yards. Edgerson may not have been able to count to five, but he was back in the game for the next play.

Rutkowski was moved to offense, and he contributed 144 rushing yards on 48 attempts, 19 receptions for 264 yards and a touchdown, and he returned 13 kickoffs for an average of 30.5 yards, which remains the highest single-season average in team history.

During the championship years of 1964 and '65 and the near championship year of '66, Rutkowski played strictly receiver and return man, often coming up with a key catch or a big return at just the right time. However, he saw his playing time curtailed in 1967, and then before the start of the '68 season he was released from the team.

"They asked me if I wanted to go with another team and I said no, I'd rather stay with the Buffalo Bills because I didn't want to move my family," said Rutkowski. "We had what they called a taxi squad at that time, so I stayed on the taxi squad. Joe Collier was coaching, and I said, 'Coach, you're making a mistake and I'm going to prove you wrong!' And I did. I got back on the team in a couple weeks. So I went from being cut before the season began to being the starting quarterback at the end of the season."

GAME DAY SETTING

It was a late August afternoon at Niagara University, which in 1968 became the new home of the Bills' training camp, and head coach Joe Collier was in an ornery mood. Three days earlier, the Bills had ventured to Tulsa, Oklahoma to play Houston in an exhibition game, and out on the prairie the Bills were stampeded, 37-7.

Now it was time to pay for those sins. Collier put the Bills through a full-contact 40-play scrimmage, his way of letting the team know that the performance in Tulsa was simply unacceptable. There were the usual grunts and groans associated with large men smashing into each other, but then came the one distinguishing yelp, the one everyone knew was just a little different.

Burly defensive end Ron McDole fell on starting quarterback Jack Kemp's right knee, bending it in a direction the knee was not built to bend. At a time before the advent of arthroscopic surgery, a knee injury meant you weren't playing any time soon. In Kemp's case, that meant the entire 1968 season, and the Bills' already remote chances for success were blown up like the ligaments in Kemp's knee.

At the time there were only two other quarterbacks on the roster: unproven veteran Tom Flores and rookie Dan Darragh, a 13th-round pick who had just completed his college career playing for Marv Levy at William & Mary. The day after Kemp was felled, Kay Stephenson joined that undynamic duo as he was acquired in a trade from San Diego.

It was a hopeless situation and Collier knew it. He chose Darragh to start the opener at home against Boston, and on the first series of the game Collier looked like a sage as Darragh marched the Bills downfield to a touchdown. By the time the Bills scored again, they had lost to the Patriots, 16-7, and were trailing Lamonica's Raiders, 34-0, in the fourth quarter of their second game.

Right around the time Darragh was throwing a touchdown pass to Bob Cappadona against Oakland to end the lengthy scoring drought, team owner Ralph Wilson was summoning player personnel director Harvey Johnson to the War Memorial Stadium press box to inform him that Collier was going to be fired and that he was taking over as coach. And no, Wilson's decision wasn't influenced by the fans in the stands derisively chanting, "Goodbye Collier, we hate to see you go!"

In less than two years the Bills had gone from two-time AFL champions and three-time East Division winners to the league laughingstock.

Over the next two months, there were games when Johnson had to use two or even all three of his quarterbacks because of injuries or inadequate play. And by late November, after Flores hurt his shoulder, Darragh hurt his ankle, Stephenson broke his collarbone, and Darragh returned but then bruised his ribs, it had come to this for Johnson: he was down to the disaster quarterback—Rutkowski.

His first start came at Denver, and Bills fans must have wondered what had taken Johnson so long to turn to Rutkowski. He hadn't started a game at quarterback since his days on the Notre Dame freshman team, but Rutkowski threw for 168 yards and when Bruce Alford kicked a 17-yard field goal with 26 seconds left, the Bills were ahead 32-31. However, Marlin Briscoe's 59-yard pass to Floyd Little after the kickoff positioned Bobby Howfield for a game-winning field goal and Denver escaped, 34-32.

Now it was on to Oakland to play the Raiders in a nationally televised Thanksgiving Day game, to play against his old buddy from Notre Dame and his former Buffalo teammate, Lamonica, to play the game of his life.

THE GAME

November 28, 1968
RAIDERS 13, BILLS 10

With only three days between games, the Bills didn't bother flying back to Buffalo and instead continued on from Denver to Oakland and practiced in the picturesque Bay Area. Not that Rutkowski saw many of the sights.

"We only had three days of preparation for the game on Thanksgiving," said Rutkowski. "So in talking to Johnny Mazur, our backfield coach, we were going over the situation and he said, 'Look, they don't think you're going to be able to do anything. They're not going to give us any complicated defenses.'

"We figured they'd use four basic defenses, and for each one of those defenses we had four offensive plays, so all I had to do was memorize 16 plays. I wrote them on my wrist and I had a little book and I took that book with me to breakfast, lunch, dinner, the bathroom, everywhere."

The Bills season was a shambles, and in fact, the fans were by now openly rooting for losses because the team with the worst record in pro football would be awarded the No. 1 pick in the 1969 draft, and the No. 1 pick was undeniably going to be Southern California's star tailback, O.J. Simpson. The Bills in the AFL and the Philadelphia Eagles in the NFL were in a neck-and-neck race for last.

Well, tough, thought Rutkowski.

"For me to play on a national holiday against my good friend and former competitor, I very much wanted to win that game," Rutkowski said.

And he very nearly won it.

From the opening whistle, it was apparent the Raiders had completely overlooked the hapless Bills, and how could they not? They had destroyed the Bills in Buffalo back in Week Two, their record was 9-2 compared to Buffalo's 1-10-1, and the Bills were starting a receiver/kick returner at quarterback.

Even Harvey Johnson questioned whether his team could compete. "If our offense doesn't do any better than it has, the score might be astronomical," he predicted.

Oakland came into the game riding a five-game winning streak and in those five games the explosive Raiders had scored 189 points, six more than the Bills had scored all season, but Rutkowski said, "Our defense played great that day. They smelled blood."

In fact, after the game Lamonica—who had become known as the Mad Bomber due to his penchant for throwing the long ball—said it was the best defense he saw all year. Raiders owner Al Davis remarked, "If the Bills could play defense only, they'd win the American Football League championship."

After playing to a 3-3 first-half stalemate, the Raiders seemed poised to run away in the third quarter when George Atkinson made a pair of interceptions against Rutkowski. The first led to a George Blanda field goal, and the second, coming just 1:07 later, Atkinson ran back 33 yards for a touchdown to make it 13-3.

At that point, the banged-up Bills and their wide receiver turned quarterback could have punched the time clock and bagged the rest of the game. They had played the Raiders tough, tougher than anyone expected, and no one back home in Buffalo could have been disappointed by the effort. Instead, the Bills had housewives from Hamburg to Lancaster trying to keep the turkey and stuffing and mashed potatoes warm because the men couldn't leave their television sets.

"You're a professional, you don't quit," said Rutkowski. "There were a couple games that year, like the game the week before against Denver, close games we should have won even with a rag-tag outfit like we had. Even though you have a losing season, as a professional you have to have pride in yourself and in your teammates, and I think we did."

Rutkowski took the Bills on a 10-play, 81-yard drive that ended with Max Anderson's five-yard touchdown run, and then he drove the Bills to the shadow of the Raiders' goal line on its next possession. Faced with a third-and-goal from the three, he took the snap, rolled out to the right side, and … "To this day I swear the ball hit out of bounds and bounced back in bounds, but they said it was a fumble," said Rutkowski.

Just before crossing the goal line for the go-ahead touchdown, Rutkowski had the ball stripped away by the ever-present Atkinson. It fell right near the sideline and Rutkowski thought it was out of bounds, meaning the Bills would retain possession. Instead, the officials ruled it landed in the field of play, and Warren Powers recovered for Oakland.

"It was kind of a naked reverse and we fooled everybody except Atkinson," said Rutkowski. "I would have made it to the end zone, but he got his arm around me. It wasn't a clean tackle, but he got his arm on the football and ripped it out of my hand. When I looked down it looked like it hit out of bounds and bounced back in, but they said it was in bounds."

The Bills still didn't quit and they had one more possession at the end of the game, but Alford missed a game-tying 48-yard field goal with less than a minute to play, and the Raiders won, 13-10.

"I had my speech all prepared," said Rutkowski. "I was going to go up to Daryle and shake his hand and kid him by saying, 'I told you I was always better than you.' But it didn't happen that way. Anyway, because of that fumble we got the No. 1 draft pick that year, who happened to be O.J. Simpson. If we had won, the Eagles would have had the No. 1 pick. And whom did they end up getting with the second pick? Leroy Keyes."

SINCE THE GAME

There was one more game to play in 1968, and it turned out to be the last game of Rutkowski's career. He started at quarterback but was relieved by Darragh as the Buffalo offense produced a grand total of 89 yards—then a franchise-low—in a 35-6 loss to Houston.

"It was a great opportunity, and I always wanted to know what it'd be like playing quarterback," he said.

And once he got a taste, he called it a career. He'd had enough of football, particularly losing football, and it was time to live the rest of his life.

Following the 1969 season his good friend, Jack Kemp, also retired, and he decided to run for Congress with Rutkowski serving as his administrative assistant. Kemp won a seat, and Rutkowski ran his office in Erie County.

He worked for Kemp for eight years, then branched off on his own when he ran for the position of Erie County Executive and won.

"Working with Jack, that's how I developed my political base," he said. "Jack wasn't available during the week because he was in Washington, so when someone needed a speaker for an event, they readily accepted me because we both sort of had celebrity status because of our football careers. That's how I developed a political following, by speaking for Jack an awful lot when he was away and couldn't get back here."

Rutkowski served as County Executive for nine years, and since leaving that post in 1987 has worked in a variety of capacities including his present job as Western District Director of New York State parks.

CHAPTER FIVE

Reggie McKenzie

Position: Offensive guard
Number: 67
Years with Bills: 1972-82
Other teams: Seahawks 1983-84
College: Michigan
Born: July 27, 1950
Birthplace: Detroit, Michigan
Current residence: Detroit, Michigan
Current occupation: President, Reggie McKenzie Foundation; Owner, Reggie McKenzie Industrial Metals

Reggie was a second-round choice in the 1972 draft by the Bills after a stellar career at Michigan where he earned All-Big 10 honors twice and was a consensus All-American playing for Bo Schembechler...played on Michigan's Rose Bowl teams in 1969 and 1971...earned All-Pro honors in 1973 and 1974...gained notoriety around the NFL because O.J. Simpson called him his "main man" during Simpson's record-setting 2,003-yard season in 1973...started 140 games in a row for Buffalo between 1972 and 1981...inducted into the College Football Hall of Fame in 2002.

THIS IS REGGIE McKENZIE

At the conclusion of the 1972 NFL season, newly crowned league rushing champion O.J. Simpson had a thought.

"If I could lead the league in rushing with the team that we had in 1972, I knew that if we improved the talent, I could do a lot better," Simpson said, remembering that despite his 1,251 yards on the ground, the Bills were weak at many positions and had finished with a poor 4-9-1 record.

Simpson wasn't sure how much better, but his best friend on the team— the ever-optimistic Reggie McKenzie—did.

"Right after the season I went to California and stayed with O.J. and his family," McKenzie said. "When I came back, I got to thinking that he gained what he gained with little or no blocking. If we could get some blocking, there's no telling what he can do. Any time he touched the football, he could go the distance. Seeing the kind of speed that this guy had and the size that he was, with any kind of blocking, we could gain 2,000 yards.

During his 11 years in Buffalo, Reggie McKenzie was one of the most popular players among fans and teammates alike. **Courtesy of Buffalo Courier-Express**

"He was talking about Jim Brown's record [1,863 yards set in 1963]. I said, 'Forget Jim Brown. Let's go do something nobody's ever done. Two grand.' He said, 'Come on, man.' I said, 'Let's shoot for two grand and really set the world on fire.'"

Setting goals and achieving them was nothing new for McKenzie. McKenzie was thrust into a leadership role almost from the day he was born in 1950. His parents, Henry and Hazel, had eight children, and they came in two waves.

"We had an older set and a younger set, and Reggie was part of that younger set," said Reggie's sister, Eleanor Blackwell.

Eleanor was part of the older group of five, and after a break along came Reggie in 1950, and then 13 months later, twins Kenneth and Keith. The last three little boys shared a bedroom in the McKenzies' house in Highland Park, Michigan, just outside Detroit, and Reggie was like the pied piper.

"Reggie was always the jokester, he always made people laugh," said Eleanor. "It was always Reggie and the twins, kind of a group of their own. When they were going to bed you could hear them giggling. My mother would say, 'Cut that out,' and Reggie would always say something funny and they'd start giggling again. He was always the leader of his little group, and we had some cousins who were that age, too, and he was always the leader of that crew."

Henry was a custodian who worked primarily in Wayne County, Hazel was a nurse, but her priority was always her children.

"My mother always found a way to make it happen," said Eleanor, who helps run the Reggie McKenzie Foundation, the youth sports organization her brother co-founded in 1974 along with former NBA player and Detroit native George Trapp.

"We sat down for dinner every night, she wouldn't have it any other way. It was a typical household, we went to church, and she was involved very heavily in the community and that's probably where we get that from."

Hazel made sure her children did not fall victim to the hardscrabble Highland Park neighborhood they grew up in. In Reggie's case that meant he was either at Cub Scout and Boy Scout meetings, or he was playing sports such as baseball, football or basketball.

Reggie excelled in football at Highland Park High School, and he earned a full scholarship to play for Bo Schembechler at the University of Michigan. He wasn't the first of the McKenzie brood to attend college, but he was the first to do so on someone else's dime.

"That was pretty big, and when he made All-American in college that was really exciting," said Eleanor. "The community had a Reggie McKenzie Day."

He played three years for the Wolverines, and from 1969-71 Michigan won 28 of 33 games, won two Big 10 titles and played in two Rose Bowls. McKenzie was a hot NFL prospect, though not quite as hot as he thought.

"I didn't know whether to be happy or sad when I was drafted," said McKenzie, who anticipated being a first-round choice but lasted until the top of the second round. "To be the first pick in the second round, well okay, I'll go to Buffalo. I was happy to be drafted because I just enjoyed playing the game and I enjoyed knocking the hell out of people. But I was coming from the University of Michigan so I wasn't used to losing."

Losing was habitual in Buffalo. The Bills had earned the No. 1 overall pick in the 1972 draft—they chose Notre Dame defensive end Walt Patulski—because of a 1-13 record. Even with the presence of Simpson, whom they had chosen No. 1 overall in 1969, Buffalo was like the Siberia of the NFL.

McKenzie started every game as a rookie, and with Lou Saban taking over as coach the Bills managed to go 4-9-1, but there was hope beyond the improved record. Saban had made it clear that he was building his offense around Simpson. McKenzie had been a key addition to the line, and when the Bills selected two more boys from Detroit—Michigan's Paul Seymour and Michigan State's Joe DeLamielleure—in the first round of the 1973 draft, McKenzie knew Simpson was destined for greatness.

And so did Simpson.

"By the time we got to camp in 1973, I saw an offense that I knew could be formidable," said Simpson.

GAME DAY SETTING

M cKenzie had played well as a rookie, forming an instant bond with the "Juice." Left tackle Dave Foley, a free agent castoff from the Jets, and 1971 draft picks Donnie Green and Bruce Jarvis had made progress at right tackle and center, respectively. Now, with Seymour and DeLamielleure added to the mix, the Bills had a young, talented group blocking for Simpson.

"The season before we kind of grew together a little bit and we felt good about the offense and the fact that the coaches were featuring O.J.," Foley said. "We felt we could move the ball on anybody."

As the preseason began, McKenzie was already on record as saying the mission was 2,000 yards, but the Bills stumbled throughout the exhibition games and lost all six, Simpson suffering a cracked rib in the process.

There were high expectations surrounding the team, not only in the locker room but throughout Western New York as the fans, having watched putrid football for so long, were genuinely excited about the team. But the dismal preseason seemed to douse the fire as the Bills flew to New England for the regular-season opener.

"The fans were panicky before the first game, but we weren't," said Green. "We didn't put much stock in our preseason record. We all got together in the hall before we boarded the bus to New England's stadium for the first game and said, 'The ball starts rolling here.'"

It never really stopped. Simpson exploded for an NFL-record 250 yards rushing in Buffalo's 31-13 victory over New England, and in just three hours the Juice was already one-eighth of the way to McKenzie's projection of 2,000.

By the time the Bills' first appearance on *Monday Night Football* was complete, a 23-14 victory over Kansas City when Simpson carried a Buffalo-

Reggie McKenzie's specialty was pulling around the end from his right guard position and leading O.J. Simpson on those memorable sweeps. **Courtesy of Buffalo Courier-Express**

record 39 times for 157 yards, he was halfway through the 14-game season and he had totaled 1,025 yards.

Lost in all the excitement was the fact that Buffalo had a 5-2 record and was in the playoff chase for the first time since the 1966 AFL season. However, a three-game losing streak to New Orleans, Cincinnati, and Miami silenced the postseason talk, and during the final month of the schedule, Simpson's quest for 2,000 yards was the focal point.

The Bills defeated Baltimore and Atlanta to improve to 7-5 and Simpson surpassed 100 yards rushing for the ninth and 10th times of the year. But with just two games remaining, Simpson was 416 yards shy of 2,000, and while Brown's record was certainly within reach, it appeared the two grand would have to wait.

Hold everything. On a snow-swept Rich Stadium field, Simpson tore through the Patriots for the second time, this time amassing 219 yards, and all of a sudden the season finale at Shea Stadium—despite its lack of playoff sizzle—was going to be one of the most watched games of the year.

THE GAME

December 16, 1973
BILLS 34, JETS 14

It was Friday afternoon, and the workday would have typically been done, but not this particular Friday. On this Friday, December 14, 1973, the members of the Buffalo offensive line—by now referred to as The Electric Company because they turned on the Juice—were working overtime.

Two days later, there was history to be made, and they were making sure they were as well prepared as possible.

"That whole season was memorable for a lot of reasons, especially the coming together of everybody," said McKenzie. "The day before we left for New York, we went in as a group, the offensive line, to watch an extra can of film after practice. We were all in there and we looked at each other, we stacked our hands in the middle and said we're not going to be denied."

The Bills flew into New York City on Saturday afternoon and the first thing McKenzie did was check the weather report. It was not promising. Cold temperatures and snow flurries were expected, and that meant the field at Shea Stadium would be very sloppy.

McKenzie was not worried. Simpson was.

Following a quiet evening in his room at a midtown Manhattan hotel, Simpson awoke from a restless night of attempted sleep with a terrible thought on his mind. As he looked out the window and saw the snow already falling, he turned to his roommate and best friend and asked "Reg, what if I only get 40 yards?"

"He was doing all of that and I looked at him and I said, 'You just gained over 200 yards against New England in a foot of snow,'" McKenzie said, reminding Simpson of his performance the previous week. "I told him, 'We're gonna get this, so you just get ready to run.'"

It was as if the gregarious McKenzie had provided a security blanket. Simpson, who later that day would attempt to break the great Jim Brown's single-season NFL rushing record and perhaps make a run at becoming the first man in history to rush for 2,000 yards, instantly relaxed.

Exactly 11 years and one day earlier, when Simpson was a teenager growing up in San Francisco, he had sidled up to Brown in a soda shop near Kezar Stadium after Brown's Cleveland Browns had defeated the 49ers to close the 1962 NFL season. The brash kid said to the superstar, "When I'm a pro I'm gonna break all your records."

Simpson didn't break all of Brown's records, but before the first quarter was through in what became a 34-14 Buffalo victory over the New York Jets, the game McKenzie refers to as the game of his life, Simpson shattered Brown's most coveted record. He followed McKenzie and Joe DeLamielleure through the left side of the line on a play called "27" for a six-yard gain, and that run vaulted Simpson past the man he would later join in the Pro Football Hall of Fame.

The appreciative New York crowd gave Simpson a standing ovation, referee Bob Frederic presented him with the ball he had carried on the record-breaking play, and his teammates hugged him and congratulated him. One particular teammate, though, wasn't satisfied. "Juice, job's not done, got lots of work to do," McKenzie said. McKenzie had set 2,000 yards as the standard and he wanted it, perhaps even more than Simpson.

"From the word go we were determined," said McKenzie. "We broke Brown's record right away and then it was, 'Let's go get the 2,000.'"

Simpson carried on seven of eight plays on Buffalo's opening possession against the Jets, gaining 57 yards to set up Jim Braxton's one-yard TD plunge for a 7-0 lead. On the play after he broke Brown's record, Simpson lost a fumble, and the Jets turned that into the tying score as Joe Namath fired a 48-yard TD pass to Jerome Barkum.

But this was Simpson's day, Buffalo's day, McKenzie's day. Simpson broke a 13-yard touchdown run with 1:12 left in the first half, and after the Jets went three-and-out on their ensuing series, Buffalo's Bill Cahill fielded Julian Fagin's low punt and roared right up the middle for a 51-yard touchdown return to give the Bills a 21-7 halftime lead.

With Simpson needing 90 yards to reach 2,000, the Bills continued to feed him the ball in the second half, but during the third quarter, the Jets defense suddenly stiffened. They had allowed Simpson to break Brown's record, they were surely going to lose the game, and they didn't want insult added to injury by letting him reach 2,000.

The Bills tacked on another touchdown plunge by Braxton and a field goal by John Leypoldt to increase their lead to 31-7, but the clock was ticking.

Early in the fourth quarter, rookie quarterback Joe Ferguson entered the huddle and delivered a progress report on exactly how close Simpson was to 2,000. Dutifully fired up, The Electric Company turned it up a notch and blew the Jets out of the way.

Simpson began ripping off chunks of yardage and eventually, knowing the record was within reach, Ferguson looked to the sideline and found out how near. Someone was holding up four fingers—four more yards—so he called Simpson's number one last time, and when New York safety Phil Wise tackled him seven yards downfield, history had been made.

"I was fired up," said McKenzie. "You look at the highlight film for that year, you see me taking the field and that wasn't speeded up, that was me taking the field in real speed. I was fired up because I had talked about it, I put it out there that we could get 2,000 yards.

"Every group has a responsibility, and ours was to block for the run, and if we did our part, we were accountable. To be able to accomplish that, to look back and say we said it and we did it and nobody can ever take it away from us, it was unbelievable. It was a great day and nobody will ever forget it."

SINCE THE GAME

McKenzie outlasted Simpson and all the members of the Electric Company as he stayed with the Bills through 1982 before being traded to Seattle where he finished his career in 1984. When he retired, McKenzie transitioned smoothly into the Seahawks' front office. During a 14-year period, he served as the Seahawks' assistant director of sales and marketing, assistant offensive line coach, director of player programs, and assistant director of pro personnel.

He had aspired to become a general manager, but it never manifested, and in 1998 he stepped away from football and returned home to Detroit to begin the next phase of his life. He started a construction management company as well as Reggie McKenzie Industrial Metals, plus spent more time working for the Reggie McKenzie Foundation.

"Coming home also gave me an opportunity to spend a couple more years with my mother before she passed away," he said.

His work at the Foundation is his most rewarding. Its mission statement is to prepare children for the future through academic excellence, athletic achievement, and by instilling self-esteem and self-confidence. Through the years, a number of well-known Detroit-area athletes have gone through the program such as Pepper Johnson, Jerome Bettis, and recently, Braylon

Edwards, and they have returned to work at McKenzie's annual football camp.

"To see the guys who participated as kids, to see them come back and now explain to the younger generation of people who are in the same position they were in, how important it is that they understand what we're trying to do is very rewarding," said McKenzie. "People who are successful didn't do it by themselves. We are all children of the dream, the product of people who sacrificed and went through struggles for us. I want to tell young people, 'I made it—you can, too.'"

CHAPTER SIX

Joe DeLamielleure

Position: Offensive guard
Number: 68
Years with Bills: 1973-79, 1985
Other teams: Browns (1980-84)
College: Michigan State
Born: March 16, 1951
Birthplace: Detroit, Michigan
Current residence: Charlotte, North Carolina
Current occupation: Celebrity greeter—Seneca Niagara Casino

Joe was inducted into the Pro Football Hall of Fame in 2003…was enshrined on the Bills' Wall of Fame in 1997…played in five consecutive Pro Bowls between 1975-79…was named a starting guard on the NFL's All-Decade team of the 1970s…won the Ralph C. Wilson Jr. Distinguished Service Award in 1987…was traded to Cleveland prior to the 1980 season and played five years for the Browns before playing one final season for the Bills in 1985…played in 185 consecutive games during his career, starting all but three.

THIS IS JOE DeLAMIELLEURE

Legendary Michigan State coach Duffy Daugherty could not believe his ears. First there was the news that the Buffalo Bills' medical staff had determined that his former star player and their 1973 first-round draft choice, offensive guard Joe DeLamielleure, might have to retire from football at the age of 22 due to a heart condition.

Then came the kicker. After the Bills' doctors had found an irregularity with DeLamielleure's ticker, they wanted to send the boy who bled Spartan green into the land of the maize and blue for a second opinion.

"Coach Daugherty said, 'No way is a Spartan going to the University of Michigan,'" DeLamielleure recalled with a wide smile. "So he got me into the Cleveland Clinic and they gave me a clean bill of health."

His was a career that was magnificent in its simplicity, wondrous in its tenacity and achievement. As an offensive lineman, DeLamielleure never garnered the spotlight, and to be honest, he never wanted it. That was left for the man he blocked for and the man he helped become one of the greatest players in NFL history, O.J. Simpson.

Instead, DeLamielleure went about his business the way any true professional would: He worked out, he studied, he practiced, he played, and then he went home to a loving wife and—by the time his career was over—six children. There were no 200-yard rushing games, no 300-yard passing games, no stats, no glory, and certainly no championships during some lean years in Buffalo.

DeLamielleure put in an honest day's work for 13 years, first with the Bills and later with the Cleveland Browns, and all he ever did was beat the living crap out of the guy in front of him, and very often, a couple other guys who happened to cross his path. It took nearly 20 years before the Pro Football Hall of Fame voting bloc realized just how good DeLamielleure was, and his career was finally afforded the proper recognition when he was inducted into the Canton, Ohio shrine in 2003.

"The hardest I ever saw Fred Dean get hit was when Joe D hit him when Joe was with Cleveland in 1984," remembered former San Francisco all-pro guard and current NFL television analyst Randy Cross. "It was our only loss of the year and they came in and smacked our defense around a little bit and a lot of that was what Joe D was doing. You don't see linemen who are impact players very often, but Joe was an impact player. He knocked out about three of our guys in that game. From an offensive lineman's perspective, to watch that was pretty special. I saw him recently at a golf tournament that Mike Ditka had, and I mentioned that to him and he knew exactly what I was talking about. He went right back to that game."

And to think, Dean and countless other defensive linemen, linebackers and defensive backs almost were spared the agony of having to face

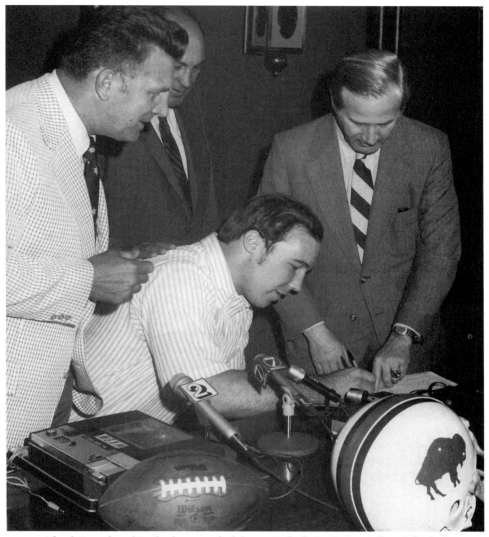

After being selected in the first round of the 1973 draft, Joe DeLamielleure's football career was put on hold because doctors thought he had a heart ailment. He happily signed his first contract with the Bills. **Courtesy of Robert L. Smith (Orchard Park, NY)**

DeLamielleure, when, for about a terrifying two-month period, it looked as if his pro career was over before it even started.

"They found an inverted t-wave, that's the medical term for it," DeLamielleure recalled more than 30 years after taking his fateful first Bills' physical examination. "It's a sign of clogged arteries. They asked me, 'Do you get dizzy? Do you ever feel light-headed?' I said no, but they flunked me anyhow, so I went back to Michigan State and Coach Daugherty said, 'There's no way there's anything wrong with you, you're the healthiest guy on this team.'

"Even today I work out like a madman, but back then I was crazy. He kicked me out of the weight room one time when I was lifting on a Saturday early in the morning before a game and he said, 'You work out too much, you're going to kill yourself.'"

Killing himself was exactly what the Bills feared following that exam, and after a while, DeLamielleure began to fear the same thing.

"I retired because I couldn't pass their physical," said DeLamielleure. "I thought I would never play again and I started to wonder how I ever played. I would imagine all these things. The news put me in a state of depression. When the Bills' doctors told me I had this problem, I believed them. I felt like I was going to have a heart attack any minute. I started to feel like I was having chest pains. You know the mind can play tricks with you. When the heart problem was first found, I accepted the doctors' decision that something was wrong. I didn't know enough about it to feel they may have been mistaken. During the weeks that followed I sat around the apartment and I actually psyched myself into believing that I was feeling some pain in the area of my heart."

He went to the renowned Cleveland Clinic, and he had the specialists shaking their heads in disbelief.

"The doctor felt my pulse, felt my ankles, and he said there's nothing wrong with you, but I have to do this procedure just to get the clearing," DeLamielleure said. "I actually set a record at the Cleveland Clinic on the treadmill and bicycle. They said, 'This guy's so healthy it's ridiculous, get off there.' I did something like running a mile in 6:20 and I weighed 254. When the doctors at Cleveland told me my heart was normal, I stopped filling my head with other thoughts. The pains suddenly went away and I haven't felt them since."

DeLamielleure broke into the Buffalo lineup as a rookie in 1973, and he made his mark right away on an offensive line that became known as the Electric Company, a group that paved the way for Simpson's NFL-record 2,003-yard season and a team total of 3,088 rushing yards, still the second best in NFL history.

During the 1970s, DeLamielleure was an All-Pro five years in a row, and he was voted as one of the guards on the NFL's all-decade team. His first three years the Bills were in playoff contention, but they made it into the postseason only once, and it was a brief appearance as they lost, 32-14, in 1974 to the eventual Super Bowl-champion Steelers.

For his final four years, the Bills struggled terribly, and when he grew disenchanted with the way coach Chuck Knox and the Bills' front office handled some player contracts and releases, he spoke his mind. It turned

into a war of words with Knox and the week before the 1980 season opener Knox traded DeLamielleure to Cleveland.

"A year after I was traded, I wanted to come back," DeLamielleure said.
"I had a lot of trouble before I was traded, but most of that was me. I was
immature at the time."

He was a solid performer for five years in Cleveland, earning a sixth Pro
Bowl invitation and two more playoff appearances, then came back to
Buffalo for one final go round in 1985 before he quietly retired when he rec-
ognized he was no longer the dominant player he had been.

On the day his name was added to the Bills' Wall of Fame in 1997, he
summed up what the game meant to him.

"The whole experience was so much more than just playing the game,"
he said. "It's the people you meet, the friendships you develop over the years.
I just had fun playing and I don't really feel I deserve anything like this. I
should be thanking you. You shouldn't be having an appreciation day for
me."

On that front, he was wrong.

GAME DAY SETTING

It was never a contest. Well, OK, for one quarter it was, as the Bills held
an early 7-3 lead against the Pittsburgh Steelers in their first-round playoff meeting at Three Rivers Stadium in December 1974.

And then the second quarter started and reality slapped the Bills across
their collective face like a jilted lover. The Steelers, not yet winners of a
Super Bowl but on the verge of winning four in the next six years, went on
a 26-point scoring barrage to open a 29-7 halftime lead on their way to a
yawning 32-14 victory.

Prior to Buffalo's first postseason appearance since the 1966 AFL championship game, the prevalent storyline was how the great O.J. Simpson
would fare against the vaunted Steel Curtain defense led by Mean Joe
Greene, Jack Lambert, Jack Ham, L.C. Greenwood and Mel Blount.

"You know Simpson is going to get his part of the pie, you just hope he
doesn't get the whole thing," said Greenwood.

Simpson got his part of the pie, but it was barely a fork's worth. In the
only playoff game Simpson would ever play, the Steelers limited him to 49
yards on 15 harmless carries, literally closing the curtain on his award-win-
ning act. It was not a banner day for the Juice, and certainly not a representative performance by the men who prided themselves on turning on the
Juice—Buffalo's offensive line.

That game chewed away at DeLamielleure throughout the winter of
1974-75. He knew how good the Steelers were. He had lived it first-hand.
He watched along with everyone else the way Pittsburgh manhandled

Minnesota in winning Super Bowl IX, limiting Fran Tarkenton, Chuck Foreman and company to 119 total yards.

"The Steelers defense, when they were on, they were unbelievable," DeLamielleure said. "If you got behind them and they knew you had to pass, forget it. If we could have run the ball against them we would have

Joe DeLamielleure was one of the greatest guards in NFL history, evidenced by his inclusion on the NFL's All-Time 1970s team and later induction to the Pro Football Hall of Fame. **Courtesy of the Buffalo Bills**

been OK, but you can't block Joe Greene if he knows you're going to pass. Joe as a pass rusher could destroy people; he could destroy lines by himself. He was incredible. That defense was as good as any defense ever, I don't care what day they're playing."

All of which made DeLamielleure and the rest of the Bills smile broadly when the 1975 NFL schedule was released, revealing a return engagement in the Steel City for the Bills. The Steelers were the measuring stick for all other NFL teams, and the Bills couldn't have been happier that in the second week of the year they would have another crack at them.

"We didn't play well in that playoff game, everyone knew we were better than that, we were better than what we showed," DeLamielleure said.

Not a lot was going to change from the December playoff game to this September showdown. The Bills were going to try to get the Juice loose, and the Steelers were going to be looking for him on every snap of the ball.

"The way O.J. runs is a gift from God," said Lambert. "Maybe one person gets it every 10 years. No question he's going to get his yards. You just have to gang tackle him, keep him from breaking the long run, and try to contain him."

That plan had worked to perfection nine months earlier. That plan blew up in their faces on a marvelously sunny afternoon in the stadium where, prior to the opening kickoff, the Steelers raised their first Super Bowl banner.

THE GAME

September 28, 1975
BILLS 30, STEELERS 21

What DeLamielleure remembers most about the game of his life is not so much the things that happened during Buffalo's stunning 30-21 manhandling of the defending Super Bowl champion Steelers, but that which happened afterwards.

"I remember talking to Jack Ham and he told me that Chuck Noll [the Steelers legendary coach] told him after that game, 'Jack, if you weren't an All-Pro I'd cut you,'" DeLamielleure said with a smile and a chuckle. "We rushed for over 300 yards that day and that was unheard of against that defense. That was their heyday, the Steel Curtain. It was just one of those days where we were great and everything clicked.

"And I remember our offensive line coach, Jim Ringo, said, 'We took the Steel Curtain apart. We kicked their ass.'"

The Bills gashed the Steelers for 310 rushing yards, including 227 by the incomparable Simpson, the fourth 200-yard game of his career, which tied Jim Brown for the all-time record.

After losing to the Bills, the Steelers went on to win their next 11 games, clinching another AFC Central title on their way to a second consecutive Super Bowl triumph. They finished eighth in the league in rushing defense, about one-sixth of the yield coming in one 60-minute epoch against the Bills. They allowed just eight rushing touchdowns, third fewest in the NFL, but couldn't stop Simpson on an 88-yard touchdown jaunt in the third quarter. The 30 points they gave up to Buffalo were just one fewer than their next four opponents scored combined. It truly was a game for the ages for the Bills.

"There was a mindset that we were going to run the ball that day, no matter what," said DeLamielleure. "No doubt about it, we were going to run the ball."

The Bills may have had the fanciest runner of the 1970s in Simpson, but nothing they did against the Steelers or anyone else was fancy according to DeLamielleure.

"Ringo was a great line coach, we had a great scheme and we'd do it over and over," he said. "We only ran about four different plays. I think it would work today. You have to have guards who can run. Everybody on that line could run a 5.0 flat except for Dave Foley. Reggie McKenzie and I were running 4.8 or 4.9 and I weighed 260. That was the key to our line. We were like the Green Bay Packers of the '60s. That's all it was; Jim Ringo came in and put the Green Bay sweep in. And once you got O.J. through the line, he was gone. In my opinion, once O.J. got through the line of scrimmage, he was the greatest runner to ever play. He was unbelievable. He ran like a guy who weighed 180, but he played at over 200 pounds."

The Buffalo defense set the tone for the day as it forced three first-half turnovers—two of which led directly to Buffalo scores as the Bills built a 10-0 halftime lead. When Joe Ferguson threw a seven-yard TD pass to tight end Reuben Gant midway through the third quarter, the Bills were on their way to a stunning victory.

Noll then benched Terry Bradshaw—the man who had guided the Steelers to a championship nine months earlier—in favor of Joe Gilliam. But Gilliam's first series ended in a punt and set the stage for one of the greatest runs of Simpson's career. On a third-and-one from the 12, Simpson took a handoff and with the Steelers bunched in tight looking for a plunge, Simpson swept out to the right, used a crushing block by Braxton on Ham, and sped 88 yards for a touchdown.

"Most backs wouldn't have gained a yard on the play he gained 88," said Noll. "O.J. is something special."

Added Steelers defensive end Dwight White: "I never played against Jim Brown, but it's beyond my wildest imagination to think he could be better than Juice."

That run was the second longest against the Steelers in their long history, second only to Simpson's 94-yard touchdown run in a 1972 game at War

Memorial Stadium. Thirty years later, those two runs remain the longest the Steelers have ever allowed.

"Nobody did that against the Steelers, ever, throughout the '70s," said DeLamielleure. "You can look at the whole decade, and no one did to them what we did to them. The Juice made many great plays, but I feel the entire offensive line enjoyed its best day. We beat the champs and we beat them in Pittsburgh, we hammered them."

SINCE THE GAME

The Bills won their first four games of the 1975 season, scoring 148 points in beating the Jets, Steelers, Broncos and Colts, and it looked as if they would go storming back to the playoffs.

Instead they lost four of their next five, including atrocious defeats against AFC East rivals Miami and Baltimore, where they blew late leads, and they finished with an unsatisfying 8-6 record, two games behind both the Dolphins and Colts.

And then came the collapse. After three years of contending for a playoff berth, the team slipped into a deep funk, prompting coach Lou Saban to quit five games into 1976.

"We were young, and back then we were foolish thinking we'd keep coming back year after year, but it's hard to make the playoffs," said DeLamielleure, who never played another postseason game for the Bills.

Forget the playoffs. During DeLamielleure's last four years in Buffalo, it was hard for the Bills to win games. They did so just 17 times in 60 tries, and just when Chuck Knox turned it back around in a positive direction in 1980, DeLamielleure was shipped to Cleveland and he missed the playoff seasons of 1980 and '81. By the time he returned to Buffalo in 1985, the Bills were back in the NFL's dungeon suffering through back-to-back 2-14 seasons.

After retirement, DeLamielleure was involved in a number of businesses in his adopted hometown of Charlotte, N.C., but one in particular stands out. He owned a restaurant and an investor named Michael Schaefer bilked him out of his life savings, about $240,000, and what he endured during that period made his brief dalliance with his pre-career heart condition seem petty by comparison.

"I had just gotten scammed, I lost my money, of course I was depressed, you'd be depressed, too," he said. "I was between homicidal and suicidal. If I had found the guy, I would have killed him. I was depressed and I thought, 'Damn, I screwed everything up.' But I made it back."

Too proud to file for bankruptcy, he battled his way out of debt and gained a slight measure of satisfaction when he helped send Schaefer to prison, wearing a wire for the FBI to catch the criminal.

DeLamielleure turned back to the game that had been his life for so long, taking a high school coaching job, and later he moved up to the college level, working under his old Browns coach, Sam Rutigliano, at Liberty College, and then for five years at Duke University.

Now selling security services for a company in Charlotte during the week and spending his autumn Sundays at Bills home games as a celebrity greeter in what very well may be the largest luxury suite in the NFL, DeLamielleure is living large as a Hall of Famer.

"One of the veteran Hall of Famers told us that our lives would be forever changed, that we would be walking on a different side of the street now," Joe D said. "It's like you've received a special stamp of approval. Things have never been better. It's been a pretty amazing journey."

CHAPTER SEVEN

Jerry Butler

Position: Wide receiver
Number: 80
Years with Bills: 1979-86
Other teams: None
College: Clemson
Born: October 12, 1957
Birthplace: Greenwood, South Carolina
Current residence: Cleveland, Ohio
Current occupation: Director of Player Programs—Cleveland Browns

Jerry was the No. 5 overall choice in the 1979 draft…earned AFC offensive rookie of the year honors that season, catching 48 passes for 834 yards and four TDs…was a track star at Clemson and won the 60-yard dash in the 1978 ACC championships…led the ACC in receptions as a junior and senior…when he graduated he was Clemson's all-time leading receiver.

THIS IS JERRY BUTLER

To most Bills fans, they are merely the names of players who once wore the helmet adorned with the charging Buffalo: Bob Chandler, Frank Lewis, Ron Jessie, Byron Franklin, Lou Piccone, and Perry Tuttle.

To Jerry Butler, they were his teammates, his friends, and his inspiration.

During the eight seasons Butler spent with the Bills, he had a tradition that served as his way of remembering and honoring departed teammates. Whenever a fellow wide receiver left the team—whether by trade, release or retirement—Butler would confiscate the nameplate above that player's locker and stick it to the inside wall of his own locker stall.

"It was kind of my wall of fame, my locker of fame," Butler said. "It was my way to pay tribute to some of the guys that had come before me, guys that I had played with and who were part of the team. That was what I did to keep them a part of my life. We were part of each other's lives when we were with the Bills. I always told them, 'You may be gone, but you aren't forgotten.' It meant a lot to me. And it helped me stay grounded and reminded me that my name could wind up on that wall if I didn't work hard and be productive."

It's a good thing Butler didn't choose to start a tradition of affixing the names of all the defensive backs he embarrassed during his much-too-brief yet still dazzling career because there simply wouldn't have been enough room.

"If those injuries had not occurred, Butler could have become a great one," former Miami Dolphins coach Don Shula once said of the track man turned fleet-footed wideout from Clemson.

Actually, Butler was a great one, but the devastating spate of injuries he endured prevented him from becoming one of the greatest. He caught only 278 passes for 4,301 yards and 29 TDs during his time in Buffalo which doesn't sound like much and will never get him into the Pro Football Hall of Fame, nor probably onto the Bills Wall of Fame.

But the numbers aren't bad when you consider Butler played the equivalent of just five and a half seasons. He missed three games his rookie year due to a shoulder injury, lost seven games in 1982 due to the players' strike, he missed half of 1983 and all of '84 due to a serious knee injury, and then he broke his lower leg midway through 1986 and never played again.

"It was disappointing, but I use those experiences to pass on to other athletes because what I lacked was a good physical foundation," said Butler, who today spends part of his days counseling players as the director of player programs for the Cleveland Browns.

"I came through Clemson not hitting the weights as hard as I should because I ran track there as well. I was always running around. Then I got

Jerry Butler enjoyed the greatest day any Bills receiver has ever seen in this 1979 game: 10 receptions for a record 255 yards and four touchdowns. **Courtesy of Robert L. Smith (Orchard Park, NY)**

to Buffalo and before Rusty [Jones, the team's strength and conditioning coach] came in we only had a little Universal area there, not much of a weight room. Things have changed a lot. I would have loved to have spent more time on the weights."

Born in tiny Greenwood, South Carolina, Butler was one of five children who grew up in the rural south in a family that had very little money. "Life was never rosy when I was growing up and I think my basic philosophy towards money came from my family," he said. "They never worried about the money they didn't have, they worried about doing things with the money they did have."

One thing Butler's parents couldn't have done was send Jerry to college, but a track scholarship took care of that. And once he arrived at Clemson, the former high school quarterback decided to play football as well.

Clemson certainly got its money's worth from the track scholarship it offered as Butler won the 60-yard dash at the 1978 Atlantic Coast Conference championships, but it was in football where Butler really shone for the Tigers.

In catching 139 passes for 2,223 yards and 11 TDs, he was the school's all-time leader in all three categories when he graduated. In both 1977 and '78 he led the ACC in receptions, and he helped lead the Tigers to back-to-back appearances in the Gator Bowl.

With two first-round draft picks at their disposal in 1979, the Bills—in need of a game-breaking receiver to team with strong-armed quarterback Joe Ferguson—used one on Butler.

Butler made an immediate impact as a rookie when he caught 48 passes for 834 yards and four touchdowns, all four of those touchdowns coming on one brilliant afternoon at Rich Stadium during a 46-31 victory over the AFC East-rival New York Jets. It was just the fourth game of his NFL career, but it was the game of his life as he caught 10 passes for an NFL rookie-record 255 yards, then the seventh best receiving yardage game in NFL history.

"I just couldn't do anything wrong that day," said Butler.

Nor did he do much wrong in 1980 and '81 as the go-to receiver when the Bills qualified for the NFL playoffs, ending a drought that extended back to 1974. Butler earned a Pro Bowl invite after the '81 season and he was destined to become a regular in the all-star game in Hawaii until the afternoon of October 30, 1983, when he caught his toe in the Rich Stadium artificial turf and shredded his knee.

He sat out the next year and a half, then made a triumphant return in 1985, though his personal satisfaction was doused by the fact that Buffalo suffered through a second consecutive 2-14 nightmare.

"In our last preseason game it dawned on me, 'Man, I go from a starter in the NFL, a Pro Bowl player, and now I'm playing in the fourth quarter of a preseason game,'" Butler recalled. "I wasn't even sure I was going to make the team. But I made it and it got down to right before the opening game against San Diego and Kay Stephenson came over to me and said, 'You're starting today.' I thought he was kidding."

Butler caught four balls for 140 yards that day and went on to catch 41 for 770 yards during that dismal year.

Jim Kelly arrived to rescue the franchise in 1986 and just when the Bills began starting to show signs of life, Butler's career came to an end. In the ninth game of the year and just the second under new head coach Marv Levy, Butler made his final reception, the kind of reception that defined what kind of player he was. He leaped between two Miami defenders to make a fantastic grab of a Kelly pass in the end zone, but when he came down, he landed awkwardly and his leg snapped.

So much talent—so much bad luck.

GAME DAY SETTING

It was shortly after draft day 1979, and Butler and his agent, Houston-based Clifford Paul, were discussing how they wanted to approach contract negotiations with the Bills.

Butler had been the fifth overall pick of the draft, but he had been Buffalo's second choice in that opening round as the team made Ohio State linebacker Tom Cousineau the No. 1 overall selection.

"We knew they were going to offer Tom a hell of a lot of money and we were afraid they might have a budget and not give us that much," said Butler. "Our whole strategy was to get to Buffalo ahead of Cousineau and sign our contract first. The figures Buffalo presented looked pretty good and the contract was decent, and we signed in a hurry."

The ink was barely dry when Cousineau revealed he was considering playing in the Canadian league because his representatives couldn't work out a deal with the Bills. Too late for Butler, and when Cousineau did eventually stiff Buffalo, the Bills had one heck of a bargain under contract in Butler.

"After Tom decided to go to Canada I looked back and wondered if I didn't blow a lot of money going in first," Butler said, laughing at the memory. "No matter how I looked at it, I really was like a second-round pick. I think the spotlight was always on Cousineau. I kind of got overlooked in that respect, but that's all right. I don't really go for the accolades. Having been drafted in the first round, that's still pretty prideful for my family and everything. I turned my attention to what I needed to learn to be the best."

He was a quick study. In his second game as a pro, the Bills blew out Cincinnati, 51-24, and Butler caught seven passes for 116 yards. Ferguson knew he had a supreme talent at wideout, and in the days leading up to the Jets game, Ferguson was licking his chops at the prospect of having Butler go against Jets rookie cornerback Johnny Lynn. Of course, Butler was also a rookie.

"Joe liked to pick on rookie defensive backs but I said, 'Hey, you have to know how to roll your dice because you've got a rookie receiver going against that rookie DB,'" Butler said. "But Joe just said, 'I can depend on you.'"

THE GAME

Sunday, September 23, 1979
BILLS 46, JETS 31

Chuck Knox would call out "Big Ben" during practice, and the Bills would roll their eyes. At least those who knew what "Big Ben" meant.

"Big Ben" was a nickname in circulation before the modern-day "Big Ben"—Pittsburgh Steelers quarterback Ben Roethlisberger—was even born.

To Knox, "Big Ben" is what most teams refer to as "Hail Mary," the desperation pass play teams try at the end of a half or a game where the quarterback launches a long throw into a cluster of receivers and defensive backs, hoping one of his guys can make a miraculous catch.

"Chuck felt better calling it the 'Big Ben' instead of the 'Hail Mary,'" said Butler. "He used to say, 'I learned that in eighth grade Sewickley.' He would say that all the time and we never knew what he meant. I'm from the south, I didn't know what that meant, but you were afraid to ask the head coach what the heck that meant. Then I found out later that's where he went to school, Sewickley, Pennsylvania."

Most of the players hated practicing the "Big Ben" because in a game situation the odds of the play working were slim to none. It seemed like a waste of time, but Knox insisted on practicing it at least once a week because, as he'd say, "You never know."

"We worked on that 'Big Ben' play all the time in practice," said Buffalo's perennial all-pro guard Joe DeLamielleure. "Somebody usually would say, 'What the hell are we practicing that play for?' And some other guy might say, 'Here we go again, now we're gonna waste five or 10 minutes on this damn thing.' But that practice sure paid off."

It had not been an impressive start for the Bills as they trailed the Jets, 24-12, and they were down to their last play of the first half, the scrimmage line their own 25.

"I had a feeling we were in trouble," said DeLamielleure. "I told the priest [team chaplain John Manion], 'It's going to be a long day if we don't do something quick.'"

They did something quick. Knox called "Big Ben" and seconds later those rolling eyes were replaced by wide eyes when the play worked to perfection and Butler scored a game-turning touchdown as the gun sounded to end the first half amid raucous cheers from the delirious Rich Stadium crowd of more than 68,000.

Butler, Frank Lewis, and Lou Piccone were all sent to the right side of the formation. The Jets reacted by bringing extra defensive backs to that side, and dropped three men into deep safety positions. Everyone knew what was coming, there was no trickery, but somehow New York botched the coverage. Instead of the Jets knocking the ball down, it somehow got popped into the air and Butler caught the deflection near the 30-yard line and sprinted the rest of the way to the end zone to complete the 75-yard play that vaulted the Bills back into the game.

"That particular game the point guy was Frank Lewis because he didn't like to run all the way to the end of the field," Butler explained with a devilish smile, poking a dig at his former teammate. "What the quarterback has to do is get it long and deep and as the point of the ball comes down it's kind of a jump ball. What happens is, the point guy tries to get up and bat it either to his left or right. He's flanked short on one side, and the other guy is a little longer on the other side of him, and that was me.

"Frank got set up, and he got ready to go up, but the DBs came over the top of him and knocked the ball away. I was probably four or five yards away looking at the crowd, and all of a sudden the ball popped out and I just ran as hard as I could and headed on in. That was a pretty neat play."

Butler's first touchdown of the day came when he beat Lynn on a quick slant and caught Ferguson's five-yard laser to cut Buffalo's deficit to 17-12. After the Jets answered with a 37-yard Richard Todd to Wesley Walker touchdown, the "Big Ben" play sent the Bills into their locker room fired up and brimming with confidence as they now trailed only 24-19.

Then early in the third quarter Buffalo took the lead for good when Butler burned the Jets' secondary for a 74-yard touchdown, his third of the game.

"It was supposed to be a screen, but I had the option of taking off depending on the coverage," said Butler. "Joe read the coverage perfectly when Lynn came up to play the screen and he laid it right out there for me. The ball was a little bit short. I remember slowing down a little bit and coming back inside, somewhat over the back of the shoulder. I think Lynn pretty much stumbled and wasn't able to recover to actually catch up with me. I swiped the ball and took it all the way in."

His fourth touchdown catch of the game came less than four minutes later when he caught a nine-yard pass from Ferguson who, with 367 yards passing, enjoyed the finest game to that point in a career that had begun in 1973.

"Every game you start out confident that you can produce something," Butler said. "Wide receivers are a little funny, and I say that because they like to get involved in the game early. Blocking is part of the game, but that's not the most exciting part. Trying to feel the leather, that's what it's all about. You have goals going into the game and I think if you get a receiver involved in a game early, it can be a positive game for you. And that's exactly what happened in that game. Joe Ferguson started right out of the box, boom, here we go, Jerry. I think that kept me wired pretty much the whole game."

SINCE THE GAME

Butler had started thinking about life after football even before injuries forced him to retire. He started Butler Construction, Inc. of WNY in 1983, and he jumped into the business full time after his retirement.

He later returned to the Bills in 1993 as director of player development/alumni relations and through his efforts he helped rebuild the team's relations with its alumni, and many former players lauded his efforts.

However, once he got back into football, his thirst to coach—something he had wanted to do after he retired—became stronger. In February of 1999, that thirst was quenched when the expansion Cleveland Browns hired him to be their receivers coach.

"It was unexpected," he said. "When I got the call from Coach [Chris] Palmer, it was out of the blue. I hadn't applied with the Browns. I guess I was the type of guy they wanted to coach their style of receivers."

Butler stayed on the field for a couple years, then moved into the Browns front office working as Cleveland's director of player programs.

Jerry Butler spikes the ball near the end zone after pulling down a Hail Mary pass against the Jets that highlighted the game of his life. **Courtesy of Buffalo Courier-Express**

CHAPTER EIGHT

Jim Haslett

Position: Linebacker
Number: 55
Years with Bills: 1979-86
Other teams: Jets (1987)
College: Indiana (Pennsylvania) University
Born: December 9, 1955
Hometown: Pittsburgh, Pennsylvania
Current residence: Destrehan, Louisiana
Current occupation: Head coach—New Orleans Saints

Jim is a charter member of the Indiana University Hall of Fame…was inducted into the College Football Hall of Fame in 2001…was selected as NFL defensive rookie of the year in 1979…was in on 763 tackles during his 90-game Bills career and also had 8.5 sacks, 11 fumble recoveries and five interceptions…was an all-AFC selection in 1980…led Bills in tackles in 1979, '80 and '85 and was second in '81 and '84…had a career-high 170 tackles in '85.

THIS IS JIM HASLETT

Beth Wood was sitting at home watching on television as the Buffalo Bills were playing the Chicago Bears in the final preseason game of the 1986 season, and the sight of Jim Haslett flashing across the screen drew her ire.

As catering manager of the Cheektowaga hotel where the Bills stayed the night before home games, Wood had seen Haslett on numerous occasions and apparently was unimpressed by the unruly Buffalo linebacker. So, when the camera panned to No. 55 she blurted out to a couple family members also watching the game, "That Jim Haslett is so obnoxious, I hope he breaks his leg."

Two plays later, that's exactly what Haslett did. Thus, the game that became a benchmark in Bills' history because it was the first one quarterback Jim Kelly ever played for the team also became the most significant game of Haslett's career for three life-changing reasons.

First, it wound up being the last game Haslett played for the Bills. Second, it spawned an unlikely love affair. Third, it re-directed Haslett's career on a new, exciting and ultimately lucrative course.

One at a time here.

Haslett sat out the entire 1986 season and his comeback ended in August of 1987 as new Bills coach Marv Levy waived him when he couldn't beat out young newcomers Shane Conlan and Ray Bentley in training camp. A few weeks later when the NFL players went on strike, Haslett tried to revive his career by signing with the New York Jets' replacement team, but after the three scab games were finished, Haslett was released and he never played again.

It was a difficult time for Haslett, but it was made easier by the woman who had wished on him bodily harm.

Feeling as if she had jinxed him, Wood sorrowfully shared the story with Buffalo punter John Kidd a couple weeks later, and Kidd couldn't resist telling Haslett. Kidd also slipped into the conversation that Wood was an attractive woman and that Haslett should give her a call. Naturally, the free-spirited Haslett thought that would be a hoot.

"John Kidd had a speaking engagement at the hotel and he came back and said, 'I met this girl, she's cute, you ought to talk to her,'" Haslett recalled. "I'm bored, I had broken my leg, so one day I called her, and I told her I heard she was a witch. She said, 'Oh, I didn't mean it that way, I apologize.' The next thing I know, I tell her since she wished for me to break my leg she needed to have dinner with me or at least go out for a drink. I ended up meeting her for a drink, and she brought an entourage with her because she was scared of me, but pretty soon I started dating her. Now we've been married 16 years and we have three kids."

Jim Haslett's baby face belied the ferocity with which he played during his Buffalo career. **Courtesy of the Buffalo Bills**

And the Haslett family—Jim, Beth, daughters Kelsey and Elizabeth and son Chase—is well-heeled and living in a New Orleans suburb because Jim in 2005 will be in is sixth season as head football coach of the Saints, a career path that through tears of pain nonetheless began coming into focus that fateful day.

While Bills trainer Eddie Abramoski and team doctor Richard Weiss were working on Haslett, then Buffalo head coach Hank Bullough came out to check on his fallen player and Haslett, knowing the injury was serious, asked Bullough for a coaching job.

"I said, 'If I can't play again will you give me a coaching job?'" Haslett recalled with a chuckle. "He said, 'Don't worry about that, you'll play next year,' and I started yelling at him, 'You've got to give me a job.'"

Haslett began his football odyssey in the suburbs of Pittsburgh, where he played quarterback and safety for Avalon High School—"Yeah, I was a quarterback who couldn't throw," he laughed—before enrolling at Indiana University.

Mind you, not the Indiana University that played big-time college football in the posh Big Ten, the Indiana University where infamous basketball coach Bob Knight used to throw chairs across the floor. No, Haslett went to tiny Indiana University near his hometown of Pittsburgh, home of the Indians, members of the Pennsylvania State Athletic Conference.

Haslett did not try out for the team as a freshman, but he had a change of heart as a sophomore and made the roster as a safety and a punter. Early in his first season, a rash of injuries hit the defensive line and Haslett—who weighed all of 180 pounds at the time—volunteered to play defensive end. "He just laughed at me," Haslett said of coach Bill Neal's response. However, Neal took Haslett up on the offer and he wasn't laughing when Haslett set a still-standing school record with 20 sacks that season.

As a senior Haslett was in on 144 tackles and had eight sacks as he earned his third straight All-America honor. He also averaged 41.5 yards per punt and that intrigued NFL scouts more than his play on defense. Buffalo scout Chink Sengel was the lone dissenter.

"Chink came down to look at me and I was punting for the Oilers," said Haslett, who by then had bulked up to 230 pounds. "Chink walked up and said, 'Do you want to punt, or do you want to play linebacker?' I said, 'I want to be a linebacker,' and he said, 'Quit punting.'"

Sengel worked Haslett out, then he left campus, and Haslett said, "I never saw him again, so I thought they weren't going to draft me. I thought Pittsburgh, the Raiders or the Saints were going to draft me, and the next thing I know Buffalo takes me. I wasn't expecting that."

Nor was he expecting the celebration that took place in Indiana after he was selected in the second round, No. 51 overall. His buddies gave him a proper sendoff as they loaded him up with beer until he passed out, then stripped off his clothes. When he regained consciousness he walked home to his apartment right down Main Street in Indiana buck naked, save for a pair of tennis shoes. "I'm glad I didn't remember it," he said.

Not that anyone who knew Haslett was surprised by the debauchery. He was definitely a wild child, and when he arrived in Buffalo, he found the perfect partner in crime in fellow rookie Fred Smerlas, a nose tackle whom Buffalo had also taken in the second round, No. 32 overall.

Haslett and Smerlas were inseparable. Bills coach Chuck Knox once said they were the "only pair I ever saw that beats a full house." Their teammates alternately called them Frick and Frack, Tweedle Dee and Tweedle Dum, Tom and Jerry or Pete and Repeat. In their first training camp at Niagara University, a television reporter tried to interview them together and within minutes, Haslett had taken the microphone and was interviewing Smerlas himself. "Why are you so ugly?" Haslett asked, to which Smerlas replied, "No one is uglier than you." The interview never made it onto the air.

Normally the rookies are hazed in camp, but Smerlas and Haslett were the hazers, not the hazees. They would call their teammates' dorm rooms at 3 a.m. and wake them up, or they'd sneak into the rooms and steal mattresses and personal belongings and hide them in a vacant room. They'd knock on a door and throw shaving cream can bombs or firecrackers into the rooms and watch with glee as the unsuspecting occupants would dance around. Filling a bed with ice was always fun, as was jamming pickles into cleats or hiding other equipment. At bed check time, they would hide in their room and when the coach doing the check entered, they'd jump out and scare him to death.

One time on an early-season road trip to San Diego, they arrived at the team hotel and found an employment agency interviewing potential airline stewardesses. Pretty soon they sat down at the table to "help" in the interview process. Back home the two would go door to door in their respective suburban Buffalo neighborhoods asking people to choose which one was the ugliest, the chosen winning a $20 bet.

They got away with their hi-jinks because both proved they could play. Haslett started immediately, Smerlas broke into the lineup midway through the year, and together with inside linebacker Shane Nelson, they formed the Bermuda Triangle, aptly named because running backs got lost when they ran up the middle against the Bills.

Smerlas wound up playing in five Pro Bowls and earned induction into the Bills Wall of Fame. Haslett did not reach those heights, but he was one of Buffalo's most reliable players, leading the team in tackles three times and earning Associated Press NFL defensive rookie of the year honors in 1979.

GAME DAY SETTING

It was late November of 1979, and Haslett had already exceeded all expectations and was well on his way to winning the NFL's defensive rookie of the year award.

Bills fans had quickly learned to love his passion and his toughness, and they really loved his off-the-wall personality. But many were having a hard time forgetting Tom Cousineau, the rookie linebacker who they thought was going to be starting on the inside of coach Chuck Knox's 3-4 defense.

"I'm sick of hearing about Cousineau," Haslett snapped one day when asked for the umpteenth time about the Ohio State linebacker whom the Bills had taken with the No. 1 overall choice in the NFL Draft six months earlier. "He was never here, he never had the job. I'm not taking anyone's place. If he shows up, he'll have to beat me out."

Given the way Haslett played as a rookie, and the way he went on to play throughout his Buffalo career, it's doubtful whether Cousineau would have ever been able to beat out Haslett.

Of course, that competition never took place—Cousineau spurned the Bills and signed with the Montreal Alouettes of the Canadian Football League, the ultimate slap in the face to the Bills and the city of Buffalo.

Cousineau was everybody's All-American, the no-doubt-about-it No. 1 pick, the can't-miss prospect who was going to rejuvenate a Buffalo defense that was sorely in need of some help after allowing the fifth most points in the NFL in 1978.

After the selection of Cousineau at No. 1, wide receiver Jerry Butler at No. 5, and then nose tackle Fred Smerlas at the top of the second round, experts were already lauding the Bills for their brilliant draft. Even though Haslett was taken in the second round, still a lofty position, he was almost an afterthought, though not to the Bills' scouting staff, led by Norm Pollom.

"At that level of competition you look for a guy who dominated the league or the competition he played," Pollom said on draft day. "That's what he did. His temperament is a lot like Jack Lambert's."

After playing defensive end in college, Jim Haslett was switched to inside linebacker when he arrived in Buffalo, and he teamed with linebacker Shane Nelson and nose tackle Fred Smerlas to form the "Bermuda Triangle." **Courtesy of Robert L. Smith (Orchard Park, NY)**

And it was that mean streak that helped Haslett make the quantum leap from small-time college football to the NFL.

"I wasn't a polished linebacker at the time and they had to keep it simple," said Haslett. "I really didn't know what I was getting into. I was supposed to be a backup and I sort of worked my way up into a starting role. Cousineau never came to Buffalo so they stuck me inside where I had never played in my life. I just kind of ran around and didn't know what I was doing, but I ended up making a lot of tackles."

Seventeen of his team-leading 143 tackles that year came in his first NFL game, a 9-7 loss to Miami, and even though the Bills lost, it was obvious the defense was vastly improved.

By the time they flew to Boston to take on the Patriots, the 6-6 Bills had already surpassed their win total of 1978, Chuck Knox's first year in Buffalo, and they were still alive—albeit barely—in the race for the AFC East title.

THE GAME

November 25, 1979
BILLS 16, PATRIOTS 13 (OT)

When the longest regular-season game to that point in Bills history was complete, quarterback Joe Ferguson asked the assembled media in the crowded visitors locker room at New England's Schaefer Stadium, "When's the last time we've been 7-6?"

Of course, the proud veteran knew the answer to his own query. It was 1975. Four years, two head coaches and so much misery ago. Seven wins in one season? During the three-year span from 1976-78 when the Bills were coached by Lou Saban, Jim Ringo and finally Chuck Knox, they had won 10 games combined.

But the sagging fortunes of the franchise had begun to turn in a positive manner during November of 1979, and on this Sunday after Thanksgiving the Bills had plenty to be thankful for as Nick Mike-Mayer kicked a 29-yard field goal to give them a 16-13 victory over the Patriots in the first overtime game in team history.

"It was the biggest game of the year, our biggest game in four years," said Ferguson, who in this game raised his passing yardage total for the season to 2,926 yards, a new Bills' record. "To beat a team of this caliber makes this one big. If we win the next three and New England and Miami lose, we could make the playoffs. It sounds ridiculous, but. ... "

In all honesty, it was ridiculous. The Bills still trailed both the Patriots and Dolphins by a game with three to play. And their remaining schedule included a home test against a 9-4 Denver team that was fighting for the AFC West title, and road games at Minnesota and defending Super Bowl-champion Pittsburgh.

There was no way Buffalo was going to the playoffs, but on that particular day, in that locker room with the sweet scent of long-awaited success lingering in the air, after the defense had held the NFL's highest-scoring offense to 13 points in 69 minutes, the Bills deserved an opportunity to dream.

"I can't remember much about the game," Haslett said of the game he chose as the game of his life, "but I do remember we were excited because we knew if we lost we were going to be out of it and we wouldn't have a chance to win the division. That was our ultimate goal. We were very excited about winning that game."

And Haslett was particularly excited because he made the first two interceptions of his NFL career, the second one coming in overtime and leading to Mike-Mayer's game-winning field goal.

"I waited 17 games for those interceptions," Haslett said, counting Buffalo's preseason games, which only a first-year player would do. "I was going for the all-rookie team, but now I'm going for rookie of the year."

A lofty goal, one he achieved, and his performance in this game was one of the keys.

Neither team could move on its first possession in overtime, but on its second foray, New England marched to the Buffalo 32 where quarterback Steve Grogan was confronted with a fourth-and-two. A 50-yard field goal was a bit out of kicker John Smith's range and punting wasn't an option, so coach Ron Erhardt decided to go for the first down. Grogan rolled out and tried to hit fullback Don Calhoun near the first-down marker, but Haslett reached out and picked it off with one hand.

"We were in a 5-2 defense to stop a run," Haslett recalled. "I saw it was a play-action so it was my responsibility to take the tight end. I saw that Butch [fellow linebacker Isiah Robertson] did a great job holding Russ Francis in. Then Shane Nelson picked Francis up. He was supposed to be my man, but I saw the back coming so I slipped inside of him, juggled the ball and caught it."

Haslett, who suffered from back spasms before and during the game yet still played and made eight tackles, returned the interception 11 yards to the 42 before Francis, New England's burly tight end, caught him. "I remember Russ Francis catching me from behind and yelling at me all the way," Haslett said.

After an incompletion and a false start penalty, the Bills were stuck in a second-and-15 hole, but Ferguson hit Jerry Butler with a 51-yard pass to the New England 12. On the next play, Mike-Mayer kicked the winning field goal, giving Knox his first victory over a team with a winning record in his brief tenure with the Bills.

Mike-Mayer had tied the game at 3-3 on the last play of the first half with a 29-yard field goal, and shortly after Haslett made the first interception of his career to thwart a Patriot advance, Mike-Mayer put the Bills ahead in the third quarter with a 26-yarder.

The Patriots moved ahead 10-6 when Grogan scored on a quarterback keeper early in the fourth, and when Smith tacked on a 32-yard field goal with 1:25 remaining in regulation the Bills' season was on the line.

Needing a tying touchdown, Ferguson produced. He marched the Bills 64 yards in just 1:08 and his 11-yard touchdown pass to Lou Piccone and Mike-Mayer's conversion with 11 seconds left sent the game into overtime, Buffalo's first venture into an extra period since regular-season overtime was enacted in 1974.

"I believe in positive thinking because it has kept me going in this league for a long time," said Piccone. "I was trying to get guys smiling in the fourth period and saying, 'Yeah, we're gonna do it, we're gonna win this game.' Anytime you go from losing to winning, you can see it. The defense saw the big plays and the offense saw guys catching the ball. We're coming together now."

SINCE THE GAME

Hank Bullough wasn't around to give Haslett a coaching job in Buffalo by the time he started looking, but Haslett wouldn't have taken it any-way.

"Marv Levy offered me a job coaching the inside linebackers [in 1988], but I didn't want to do it because these were the guys I had just hung out with and played with and it would have been uncomfortable," said Haslett.

Haslett also turned down offers from the San Diego Chargers and Indianapolis Colts because, despite his pleadings to Bullough, he wasn't quite sure if coaching was the direction he wanted to go.

Serving as the perfect test laboratory was the University at Buffalo, a local Division III school that has since elevated its program to Division I. Talk about starting at the bottom and working your way up. Haslett was hired to coach the linebackers in 1988, and then he was promoted to defensive coordinator for 1989 and '90.

"I ended up going to UB and it was a good way to see if this was something that I really wanted to do, and I've been doing it ever since," he said.

He left UB to work for one of his former Bills head coaches, Kay Stephenson, who was running the operation for the Sacramento Surge of the World League of American Football. Two years in the NFL's developmental league were followed by stints with the Los Angeles Raiders and Saints before a triumphant return home to Pittsburgh to serve as defensive coordinator for Bill Cowher's Steelers.

Success at Pittsburgh led to a number of head coaching interviews, and after being rejected by Chicago, Baltimore, Seattle, and Green Bay, Haslett was finally hired in New Orleans. Despite some rough waters in the past few years, he remains in the Bayou.

"More than anything I was excited about the opportunity, but everyone was telling me I was crazy for coming down here because of the tradition, they can't win, they don't know how to win and everything," said Haslett.

In his first season he led the Saints to the playoffs and a first-round upset of the defending Super Bowl-champion St. Louis Rams at the Superdome, the franchise's first playoff victory.

Mediocrity has marked the last four years in New Orleans as the Saints haven't been back to the playoffs and have a record of just 32-32, but Haslett—whose job was in jeopardy at the end of 2004—was optimistic heading into 2005.

And if it shouldn't work out in New Orleans, there will be other jobs for Haslett because he is a solid coach, a proven winner, and a man who truly enjoys what he does.

CHAPTER NINE

Joe Ferguson

Position: Quarterback
Number: 12
Years with Bills: 1973-84
Other teams: Lions (1985-86), Buccaneers (1988-89), Colts (1990)
Born: April 23, 1950
Birthplace: Alvin, Texas
Current residence: Ruston, Louisiana
Current occupation: Commercial real estate agent and high school football
coach

Joe ranked as Bills all-time leader in completions, attempts, yards and TD passes when he left the team and still ranks second in all four categories behind only Jim Kelly...his 12 years with Buffalo ties him for the sixth-longest tenure in team history...his 508 pass attempts in 1983 stood as the team mark until Drew Bledsoe broke it in 2002...his 38 completions and 55 attempts against the Dolphins in 1983 remain single-game team records, and his 419 yards that day was No. 1 until Bledsoe broke that record in 2002.

THIS IS JOE FERGUSON

Joe Ferguson couldn't help but daydream a little on the day he returned to Rich Stadium to receive the Ralph C. Wilson Jr. Distinguished Service Award.

It was late in the 1991 season; the Bills were coming off their first AFC Championship and on their way to the second of the four in a row they would win.

That year was also when the team switched its offensive philosophy exclusively to the hurry-up, no-huddle approach, and Jim Kelly and company went on to set team records for points, touchdowns, first downs, passing yards and total yards.

As Ferguson watched his old team carve up the New York Jets that December afternoon, he watched with envy as Kelly marched up and down the field, creating havoc on nearly every possession.

"I wish we would have used it back in the early '80s," Ferguson said. "It would have been fun. I think we would have put an awful lot of points on the board."

Kelly was still in grammar school when Ferguson began wearing No. 12 for the Bills in 1973.

Ferguson had enjoyed a standout career at the University of Arkansas, earning all-Southwest Conference and league MVP honors as a junior while playing for the legendary Frank Broyles, prompting the Bills to choose him in the third round of the 1973 draft.

He was thrust into the starting role as a rookie and he spent the vast majority of time handing off to O.J. Simpson as the Juice set the single-season NFL rushing record of 2,003 yards, but gradually Ferguson began to contribute more to the Buffalo offense. In 1975 he threw 25 touchdown passes to tie for the league lead, but during the miserable years following Lou Saban's resignation as coach, Ferguson grew frustrated by the restraints placed on him.

"We weren't doing what other teams were doing, but we weren't a very good football team a few of those years," Ferguson lamented. "We had some protection problems, we didn't have the talent that some of the other teams had that were turning their quarterbacks loose. So you understand a little of why we didn't do it, but yet in your mind you were wishing you were able to see if it could have helped the football team."

The arrival of Chuck Knox and his offensive coordinator, Kay Stephenson, signaled a new beginning in 1978.

"You could tell tremendously when he first got there that he was going to be a very organized head coach," Ferguson said.

Transforming the Bills from disgraceful to competitive took a year, and Knox proceeded slowly with Ferguson during that 1978 season, but in

Joe Ferguson played gallantly on many poor Buffalo teams, and his struggles were never more noticeable than when the Bills played Miami—victories over the powerful Dolphins were priceless. **Courtesy of the Buffalo Bills**

1979, he allowed Ferguson—by then heading into his seventh NFL campaign—more leeway in the passing game. Ferguson responded by throwing for a career-high 3,572 yards as the Bills improved to 7-9.

"For so long he had handcuffs on, under different systems and coaches afraid to throw and he had to deal with that attitude of 'Whatever you do, don't throw an interception,'" said Ferguson's favorite receiver in the 1970s, the late Bobby Chandler.

In 1980, ironically after Chandler had been traded to Oakland, everything fell into place for the Bills. Ferguson had the benefit of two outstanding receivers in Jerry Butler and Frank Lewis, a playmaking running back in rookie Joe Cribbs, a bruising fullback in Roosevelt Leaks, a reliable tight end in Mark Brammer, and an offensive line that included Conrad Dobler, Reggie McKenzie, Will Grant, Joe Devlin and Ken Jones.

Oh, what the Bills could have done in the no-huddle.

"With the receivers we had who could get downfield, and the backs that we had, I wish we could have done it," he said. "We started doing the shotgun when Chuck and Kay came in. That was new, only a few teams like Dallas were doing it, and it was good for us because we had the right personnel, but I wish we would have done it more, and run it quicker."

Ferguson guided the Bills to playoff appearances in 1980 and '81, and then it was downhill from there, and after the 2-14 debacle of 1984, Ferguson was dealt to Detroit the following spring in a draft day trade.

"I still look back at those years from time to time and wonder 'What if? What if?'" Ferguson said of his 12 years in Buffalo that went largely unfulfilled. "Naturally I would have liked to have left on a happier note. I had more good times than bad in Buffalo, but that ending left me and many people with a sour taste."

GAME DAY SETTING

On opening day of the 1980 season, Ferguson enjoyed what was then the most satisfying victory of his career when he overcame a five-interception nightmare to help lead the Bills to a 17-7 victory over the Miami Dolphins.

That day the Bills snapped their NFL-record 20-game losing streak against the Dolphins, a drought that had encompassed the entire decade of the 1970s.

Ferguson had made 13 career starts against Miami and he was a perfectly brutal 0-for-13 until that gloriously sunny Sunday when the rabid Buffalo fans tore down the goal posts in celebration.

"The relief of finally beating the Dolphins was tremendous," he recalled. "It wasn't that good of a ballgame for me that day statistically, but for us to come around and beat them late in the game, it was like somebody took the Empire State Building off your back. It was such a great relief to be able to say we finally beat the Dolphins."

But that wasn't the end of Ferguson's misery against the Dolphins. Over the next three years Ferguson failed to lead the Bills to victory in the games played at Miami, extending a franchise dry spell to 16 years, of which Ferguson had been the loser nine times.

And after Miami began the 1983 season with a 12-0 victory over Ferguson and the Bills at Rich Stadium, there was no reason to believe Buffalo would end its losing ways at the Orange Bowl five weeks later.

Two players who openly admitted Ferguson wasn't up to the task were Miami's Doug Betters and Gerald Small. In the season opener Miami had picked off Ferguson twice, both turnovers leading to field goals, and sacked him six times, prompting Betters and Small to question Ferguson's poise.

"Certain quarterbacks panic when they're under pressure," Small had said. "Ferguson is that way. We wanted to keep him on the hot seat."

Added Betters: "We wanted to get Ferguson under the gun early because then he starts hearing those footsteps. He started getting a little gun shy back there and losing his concentration. We got him a little jumpy. It looked like he got a little scared out there."

Ferguson remembers being personally stung by those comments, but it wasn't Betters and Small who drew his ire so much as it was his own boss, Bills owner Ralph Wilson.

"I vaguely remember the comments they made, I know there were some, but you try not to let that bother you," he said. "But I'll tell you what happened the night before the game and nobody knows this because I've never told anyone, but I guess it's OK to talk about it now. We were down there in Miami, and I was out to dinner with some of my teammates; and Mr. Wilson was at the same restaurant. I love Mr. Wilson, he's done a lot of things for me, but he was at a table not far from us and I overheard some comments that were made about our team that night that really hacked me off."

Wilson, unaware that his players were seated close to him, apparently expressed some frustrations over the way the team had been playing. While he never intended that his words would reach the ears of his players, they unknowingly did.

Based on what happened the next day when Ferguson played the game of his life and the Bills snapped their road losing streak at Miami with a thrilling 38-35 victory, perhaps Wilson should have stood before his players every week and bad-mouthed them.

"That night I was up all night just mad about some of the things that were said," recalled Ferguson. "I didn't say anything to the team about what had been said. I'm not trying to be negative toward Mr. Wilson, he was always very good to me, and I love the guy, but that one night he made me mad, and that next day I guess I just played harder. I tried to play mad the rest of the season, but it didn't work as well as it did that day."

THE GAME

October 9, 1983
BILLS 38, DOLPHINS 35 (OT)

There were times when Ferguson drove Bills fans crazy with his habit of drooping his head when things didn't go right.

Perhaps it wouldn't have been so noticeable, so irritating, if the head-hanging was a once-in-a-while thing, but let's face it, his 12-year career encompassed an era in Bills history during which things didn't go right an inordinate amount of the time.

It's a shame that while Ferguson departed Buffalo as the Bills all-time leader in every major passing category, his robust numbers—now rendered obsolete by the man who inherited his No. 12 jersey, Jim Kelly—have always been overshadowed by that one flaw in his character. Rather than the classic mechanics, the powerful right arm, and the tightly wound spirals he unfurled, Ferguson's enduring legacy is that of the quarterback with the perpetually bowed head.

There was one occasion, though, when Ferguson could be forgiven for staring at his shoe tops because, frankly, on a steamy South Florida afternoon 22 Octobers ago, he wasn't the only member of the Bills doing it.

As kicker Joe Danelo lined up a potential game-winning 36-yard field goal, a kick that would end Buffalo's ghastly 16-game losing streak at Miami's Orange Bowl and cap Ferguson's greatest day as an NFL passer, Ferguson, some of his teammates, and Bills fans everywhere, couldn't bring themselves to lift their chins from their chests.

"I couldn't look," Ferguson said. "I told Rosey Leaks to tell me what happened."

What a story Leaks had to tell. Danelo's kick sailed through the uprights on a glorious arc, delivering to the Bills a thrilling 38-35 overtime victory over the arch-rival Dolphins while securing the most noteworthy triumph of Ferguson's career and spoiling the first professional start for Miami rookie quarterback Dan Marino.

"I feel as good as I've ever felt," he said that day. "It's taken me 11 years to win here in Miami and it's a great win for us. This is something I really wanted to do before I got out of football. It was the most emotional game I've ever played in. I'm happy for everybody, especially Joe Ferguson."

Ferguson set single-game Bills records for completions (38) and attempts (55) that remain intact today, and his 419 yards went unsurpassed until 2002 when Drew Bledsoe threw for 463 yards in an overtime victory over Minnesota. Also, Ferguson's five touchdown passes tied his own team mark set four years earlier, later broken by Kelly who threw six against Pittsburgh in 1991.

"It would have been a great win for us. Instead, it's a great win for Buffalo," said Miami coach Don Shula, whose defending AFC champions lost for the third time in six games. "Ferguson just played so well, he had all the answers."

He began providing those answers right away as he led the Bills to a 14-0 lead by early in the second quarter on the strength of a pair of touchdown passes to Byron Franklin covering nine and 30 yards.

Marino—who threw for 322 yards, the first of his NFL-record 63 300-yard games—was up for the challenge Ferguson had created. By the end of the third quarter, the score was tied at 21 and then the game really began to heat up.

Ferguson's four-yard TD pass to Joe Cribbs was matched by Marino's two-yard TD pass to Nat Moore with 7:35 left. Then, after Ferguson threw his only interception, Marino gave Miami its first lead when he hit Mark Clayton on a 14-yard slant with 3:06 left to play.

"I thought our defense would hold and we'd go home happy," Clayton said.

Ferguson would not oblige. He completed nine of 12 passes—the biggest a 20-yard connection with Franklin on a third-and-16 play—during a marvelously clutch 80-yard march that culminated in his one-yard flip to Cribbs with 23 seconds remaining. Danelo's conversion sent the game into overtime.

"No way we win that game unless he has the kind of day he had," said Buffalo center Will Grant of Ferguson.

Then again, for all Ferguson had done, the Bills still would have lost if not for a pair of errant field goal attempts in the overtime by Miami's usually reliable Uwe von Schamann, one from 52 yards, the other from 43.

It was after the second miss that Ferguson positioned Danelo for the winning kick, and he got some help from a highly unlikely source. Little-used receiver Mike Mosley was sent into the game for the first time on offense—he had been returning kickoffs during the day—and on the only pass pattern he ran, he made a 35-yard catch in a third-and-10 situation that moved the ball to the Miami 29.

"They put me in because all of our other receivers were getting tired," Mosley said, referring to the stifling 81-degree heat that had drained the Buffalo receiving corps. "When coach said, 'You're in,' I couldn't believe it. I didn't think I'd play at all. It was the first time I played the 'Z' position, but it's not too hard when all the coaches tell you is 'Run straight down the field.'"

Mosley ran straight, Ferguson fired, and as beaten Miami cornerback Fulton Walker said, "I thought I had him covered, but it was a perfect pass and a perfect catch. There was nothing I could do."

Three running plays later—with just 1:02 remaining—the outcome hinged on the right foot of Danelo, who had shanked a 27-yard attempt late in the first half.

"I was thinking, 'OK boys, this is it,'" Danelo said. "The kick was incidental after Ferguson's pass to Mosley. Without that play there's no kick. As soon he [long snapper Justin Cross] snapped it, I knew it was good. But I'm no hero."

No, that was Ferguson's role, and Miami's Doug Betters—held without a sack after getting four in the previous game—had to concede that point. "Ferguson just took us apart," he said.

SINCE THE GAME

After retiring as a player in 1990 Ferguson spent two seasons as an assistant coach at Louisiana Tech, and after going into the real estate business, he got back into football in 1996, joining the staff at his alma mater, Arkansas, where he served as quarterbacks coach for four years.

In the summer of 2004, Ferguson, his wife, Sandi, daughter, Kristen, and son, Joe, moved to Ruston, Louisiana, where Ferguson is back working again in commercial real estate while serving as the offensive coordinator for the football team at Ruston High School.

But his former Buffalo teammate, Pro Football Hall of Fame guard Joe DeLamielleure, knows what Ferguson should be doing instead.

"That's a guy who should be coaching at a higher level," said DeLamielleure. "Joe's the most knowledgeable guy I've ever met in football. He knows the game inside out. I learned how to be a coach in high school and college from Joe Ferguson. He was a dedicated player, the most competitive guy I ever played with. Everyone said he hung his head. He didn't hang his head, his head may have gone down but his mind never went down. He was always trying to figure out ways to win."

Ferguson admits the coaching bug still gnaws at him, which is why he accepted the position at the local high school. He knows breaking into the NFL fraternity is extremely difficult, but in the same breath, for a man with 18 years of playing experience, it shouldn't be as difficult as it has proven to be.

"It's tough to get into the league, and once you get in and meet people, you kind of stay in it," he said. "You would think a quarterback with 18 years experience would get a call, but I haven't. I've moved past it, but it was frustrating when you're going through it. You'd think somebody would call and at least talk to you. There's a movement to hire younger people in the NFL, but when you see some of the teams hiring quarterback coaches who never played the position, that's frustrating."

When he was traded from Buffalo prior to the 1985 season, Ferguson was the franchise's all-time leading passer. **Courtesy of Buffalo *Courier-Express***

CHAPTER TEN

Kent Hull

Position: Center
Number: 67
Years with Bills: 1986-96
Other teams: None
Born: January 13, 1961
Birthplace: Ponotoc, Mississippi
Current residence: Greenwood, Mississippi
Current occupation: Cattle farmer

Kent became a member of the Bills' Wall of Fame in 2002…earned three consecutive Pro Bowl nominations between 1988-90…was a starter for four years at Mississippi State and the Bulldogs earned a pair of bowl game invitations and top-20 season-ending rankings while he was there…began career with the New Jersey Generals of the USFL and after three years came to Buffalo when the league folded…started 121 straight games, and started 188 of the 189 career games he played in Buffalo counting the playoffs.

THIS IS KENT HULL

It was quite a caravan driving down the New York State Thruway from Buffalo to Fredonia that mid-August afternoon in 1986. Jim Kelly—who earlier that day had signed a multimillion-dollar contract with the Buffalo Bills three years after the team had drafted him—was riding in a stretch limousine, accompanied by Bills' general manager Bill Polian.

Behind the limo, there was a team equipment van, and one of its passengers was Buffalo's new center—the man who would end up hiking the ball to Kelly for the next 11 years. At the time, he was an unknown USFL castoff by way of Mississippi State named Kent Hull who accepted a $13,000 signing bonus to chase his NFL dream.

"I came in on a private jet, they picked me up in a limo and I had a police escort," Kelly recalled nearly two decades later. "Kent jumped in the back of the equipment van and he was riding with the tackling dummies following our motorcade. We came in at the same time, but it was pretty different."

When they retired from pro football a month apart following the 1996 season, they exited the same way. Kelly announced his retirement during an event held inside the Bills' practice facility that was broadcast live on local TV and ESPN. Hull said goodbye in front of a small group of reporters with hardly any fanfare in the tiny environs of the team's media room.

Marv Levy has said it often, including the day he presented Kelly for induction into the Pro Football Hall of Fame, that Kelly was the greatest player he ever coached. On the day Hull announced his retirement from the NFL, Levy said simply, "I can say with a great sense of pride that I coached Kent Hull."

Kelly, running back Thurman Thomas, and wide receiver Andre Reed grabbed the headlines and sound bites and piled up the gaudy statistics during the era of Buffalo's wildly exciting no-huddle offense, but—make no mistake—Hull was the foundation upon which all of that success was built.

"To me, he was the key ingredient to why the no-huddle worked," said Kelly. "You can talk about me, Thurman, Andre or whoever, but he was the key. He had to call all the plays on the offensive line. There were times he would turn around and tell me to get out of [a play]. He was a major, major part of the whole thing."

Growing up in the Mississippi Delta, Hull dreamed of playing basketball. His father, Charles, who went on to become Mississippi's director of agriculture, was an all-Southeastern Conference forward for Mississippi State and young Kent would spend hours shooting hoops in the driveway hoping to become the player his dad was.

Kent Hull anchored the Bills' offensive line for 11 years, earning three Pro Bowl invitations. His ability to make calls at the line became a major factor in the success of the no-huddle offense. **Courtesy of the Buffalo Bills**

"It's funny," he said. "I hated football when I was young. I wanted to play basketball. I followed basketball my whole life."

He was the star of the Greenwood High team and Division I schools came to see him with scholarship offers in hand. But Hull also had a knack for playing football, particularly after he switched from quarterback to center his senior year because "My feet got too big. I went through a really big growth spurt. I got too slow."

His football coach, Hollis Rutter, boiled Hull's decision down to numbers. "He told me, 'Son, it takes 22 to start in football and five in basketball.' He said, 'You're a good enough athlete, you'll find somewhere to play.' So I signed for football at Mississippi State. I figured I'd try it a year. If it didn't work out, I'd go somewhere else."

It worked out just fine. He was fifth string when practice began his freshman season, third string by the time the first game was played against Florida, and when the first- and second-stringers went down against the Gators, Hull wound up playing his first game as a raw freshman. Over the next four years, he never came out of the starting lineup.

No one paid attention to him in NFL circles and he went undrafted, but the New Jersey Generals chose him in the seventh round of the USFL draft and it was off to Orlando, Florida for a grueling training camp.

"You didn't know whether it was Sunday or Friday or Tuesday," Hull recalled of the brutal two-a-day sessions that went on just about every day. "I actually thought about quitting, that's how bad it was."

After a lecture from his father ended any thought of quitting, he went on to make the team and he pass-protected for Doug Flutie and opened holes for Herschel Walker. Hull centered every snap during the three-year existence of the Generals, and when the USFL folded in the summer of 1986, nine NFL teams inquired about his services.

He chose Buffalo, but didn't bother bringing his wife, Kay. "I told her they were going to cut me after six weeks," Hull recalled. Instead, five days after his arrival, as Buffalo was playing its third preseason game, he moved into the starting lineup and never left, earning three Pro Bowl nominations along the way.

"I faced the guy every day in practice from 1986 when he came to Buffalo from the USFL to 1989, and I was lucky to have anything left by Sunday," said Bills nose tackle Fred Smerlas.

Hull and Kelly came to Buffalo together. They left together. And forever more they will remain linked together as both their names are affixed to the façade of Ralph Wilson Stadium on the Bills' Wall of Fame.

GAME DAY SETTING

He was one season and two games into his NFL career and Hull was wondering if his dream of becoming a cattle farmer was going to become fulfilled a whole lot sooner than he thought.

In September of 1987, the NFL Players Association and the NFL Management Council could not come to terms on a new Collective Bargaining Agreement, so the players traded in their helmets and pads for picket signs and nasty dispositions.

"It was a scary time because we didn't know if we'd have jobs," Hull said.

Deep down the players did not want to go on strike, not even Buffalo team leaders Fred Smerlas and Joe Devlin, but once union chief Gene Upshaw and his executive committee made the decision to strike, Smerlas and Devlin knew the Bills had to stand behind the union and hit the picket line. And just as important as supporting the union, the Bills had to support themselves. They needed to stay in Buffalo, practice on their own and make sure they were ready to play (if and when) the strike ended.

The Bills hadn't done that in 1982. As that 57-day strike dragged on, they slowly drifted their separate ways and, after a 2-0 pre-strike start, the Bills returned from their eight-week vacation ill-prepared to play and lost five of seven games, failing to qualify for the postseason tournament.

Back in 1982, the striking players naturally lost money, but most did not fear long-term for their jobs, because all the games were cancelled and ultimately, the owners were losing money, too. Everyone knew there would have to be a compromise at some point, and there was.

The strike of 1987 was a bit different. This time the owners moved forward with the schedule using replacement players, and after a one-week cancellation of games, the NFL was open for business. The product was pathetic, the crowds were sparse, but there was football on Sundays and rather than playing, guys like Hull spent their time harassing the scabs who were parading around as the counterfeit Bills.

For about three weeks it looked as if the strike was going to last forever and players like Hull who had just broken into the NFL were justifiably scared about their futures. But common sense finally prevailed, the strike was called off after 24 days—without free agency being granted—and the players returned to work to pick up where the scabs left off.

The counterfeit Bills lost their first two games to the groups of imposters fielded by Indianapolis and New England, and then in their swan song they pulled out a 6-3 victory over the New York Giants despite the presence of strike-buster Lawrence Taylor.

"If anyone can pick up where they left off, we should be able to because I think out of all the teams, we probably had as many people practicing every day during the strike," said guard Jim Ritcher. "We had practices in '82 and they weren't anywhere near as productive as these were."

THE GAME

October 25, 1987
BILLS 34, DOLPHINS 31 (OT)

Buffalo's strike practices may have kept the Bills in football mode, but they in no way replicated what takes place during a normal regular-season week, and looking back on the game of his life, an improbable 34-31 come-from-behind overtime victory over Miami, Hull recognized this.

"We were just coming off the strike and we were out of shape," he said. "We felt like we were working out, but we weren't doing a very good job."

And that fact hit Hull and his teammates as soon as they stepped on the field at steamy Joe Robbie Stadium in Miami for their AFC East showdown against their fiercest rival.

"We go down there, it's in the 90s and the humidity is bad," said Hull. "And I look around and all the offensive linemen were substituting except me. But I was lucky enough that I had a guy in front of me for Miami named Bob Baumhower who was as tired and sick as I was. We'd stand there and hold each other and throw up on each other."

It took the Bills a full 30 minutes to realize they were back to work. Miami took the hint a little earlier and sprinted to a 21-3 halftime lead behind three touchdown passes by Dan Marino. Scott Norwood's 41-yard field goal on the final play of the half seemed rather inconsequential at the time as the Bills trudged to the locker room desperately seeking air conditioning and oxygen.

"We had been kind of priding ourselves during that strike that we were conditioning ourselves and still doing the things we needed to do in order to win, but we weren't prepared for that heat, I can promise you that," Hull said, shaking his head.

Despite the huge deficit, the talk in the locker room was upbeat. Kelly had that effect on people. He never felt he was out of a game, no matter what the score, no matter how much time was left on the clock.

"We were down 21-3 at halftime, we went out and we sucked it up and Jim had a great second half and we ended up winning," said Hull.

The Bills took the second-half kickoff and moved efficiently but Norwood missed a 42-yard field goal. After a Miami punt, Kelly—who would finish the day with 359 yards passing—went back to work and his 33-yard pass to Chris Burkett set up Robb Riddick's one-yard touchdown run to make it 21-10.

Another Miami punt was followed by another Buffalo touchdown, this one a 14-yard Kelly strike to Burkett and now it was the Dolphins who were sweating, literally.

"I think they were just more out of shape than we were from the strike," said Hull.

A Fuad Reveiz field goal bumped Miami's lead to 24-17, and it looked as if the Dolphins had regained control when their defense forced a Buffalo punt on the ensuing possession. However, Miami's return man, Scott Schwedes, fumbled when he was drilled by Steve Tasker, and Adam Lingner recovered at the Miami 32. On first down, Kelly threw a 29-yard pass to Andre Reed, and Riddick plowed in from the one to tie the game with 7:13 left in regulation.

Schwedes then coughed up the kickoff on a hit by Ray Bentley and Scott Radecic fell on the loose ball at the Miami 33. Five plays later, on a third-and-5 from the 17, Kelly found Riddick in the left side of the end zone for the go-ahead touchdown with 4:04 to go.

Of course, that was way too much time for Marino, and he needed less than three minutes to answer. With 1:19 remaining, he converted a do-or-die fourth-and-10 pass to Mark Duper, and on the next snap, he found Mark Clayton for the game-tying touchdown, giving him 303 yards passing.

Now came the biggest moment of the day. The overtime coin flip.

"Thank God I called tails," said Devlin.

Reveiz kicked the ball out of bounds to give Buffalo a nice drive start at its 35, and Kelly completed a pair of 18-yard passes to Reed and Burkett, moving the ball deep into Miami territory. After Riddick converted a third down, the Bills eventually drove to the 10 from where Norwood was called on to kick a game-winning 27-yard field goal that he nailed dead center.

Buffalo had lost 20 games in a row to the Dolphins in the 1970s. It had lost six in a row and nine of its last 10 to Miami. But this was the start of a new era for the Bills.

"At that time they had been whupping the snot out of Buffalo for quite some time and we hadn't had much luck with them," said Hull. "We got down there and we outplayed them. It took two halves to do it, but we did it, and I'll never forget that. Our guys were just as tired as their guys, but we were putting more into it than they were and that's why we won. That was a big turnaround for that football team. Miami didn't want to see us anymore after that year."

SINCE THE GAME

Injuries began to slow Hull in his final years, and he thought about retiring after 1993 and after 1994, but he stayed through the 1996 season. His last game was his old buddy Kelly's last game, a playoff loss to Jacksonville.

"It's been a great ride," Hull said when he announced his retirement. "I had an opportunity to play with Hall of Fame players, Hall of Fame coaches, and without a doubt, for the greatest fans in the world."

And with that, he packed up his family and headed home to Mississippi to start phase two of his life: As a farmer, chasing about 600 head of cattle around a 2,000-acre site he and his father have owned for years.

However, Buffalo still holds a special place in his heart, the 11 years he spent there that he will never forget. When his name was added to the Bills' Wall of Fame in 2002, Hull shared his feelings about the city and its football team.

"Buffalo was so much like where I live right now in Mississippi with the exception of the snow," he said. "And to think that my name will be on that stadium—I know that's my home now and it feels great. It means a great deal to me to know that the people in Buffalo are what made the Buffalo Bills in those glory days. I can look back and say, 'You know, I'm still in Buffalo because I'm on that wall.'"

Kent Hull earned the distinction of being one of the classiest men to ever wear a Buffalo Bills uniform. **Courtesy of the Buffalo Bills**

CHAPTER ELEVEN

Cornelius Bennett

Position: Linebacker
Number: 55, 97
Years with Bills: 1987-95
Other teams: Falcons (1996-98), Colts (1999)
College: Alabama
Born: August 25, 1965
Birthplace: Birmingham, Alabama
Current residence: Atlanta, Georgia
Current occupation: Retired player

Cornelius was picked No. 2 overall in the 1987 draft by the Colts, but never joined the team and Bills acquired him in one of the biggest trades in NFL history later that year…earned five Pro Bowl invitations…is the Bills' record-holder with 18 fumble recoveries…his 52.5 career sacks rank third on Bills' all-time list…had four-sack game vs. Philadelphia in 1987 that is still tied for the team record…his 80-yard touchdown return with a blocked field goal is longest in team history…played in four Super Bowls with the Bills and one with the Falcons, but was never on the winning side.

THIS IS CORNELIUS BENNETT

Cornelius Bennett could always deal with the criticism about his performance on the field.

Not that there was much of it during a superlative 13-year career that saw him participate in five Super Bowls, earn five trips to the Pro Bowl, and cobble together a resume that qualifies him as a borderline candidate for enshrinement in the Pro Football Hall of Fame.

But occasionally he'd miss an open-field tackle; and sometimes he'd use an improper technique on a pass rush maneuver that allowed a quarterback to complete a big pass; or perhaps he'd drop an interception or muff an attempt to recover a fumble. Ask him what happened and he'd admit the mistake if it was his. He'd say that's all part of football. There's a new play every 40 seconds and if you happen to have one bad down, you come back and try to excel on the next.

That's what Bennett always did. He always tried—on every play.

However, that was not the perception during Buffalo's tumultuous 1989 season, a year in which Bennett looked like half the player he had always been because, in fact, he was half the player he had always been.

Hampered by a sore knee and more prominently a painful shoulder injury that severely reduced his effectiveness, plays that he once made so routinely became an exercise in futility. "It was the first time I really struggled to play the game," he said.

Fans and media in Buffalo, unaware that he was in such physical distress because he was too proud to gripe about his ailments in public, rode him hard and wondered aloud if Bennett—the supposed second coming of Lawrence Taylor—was grossly overrated.

It was the worst football season of his life. Not in Pop Warner, not in high school, not in college, and not before or after in the NFL had he experienced anything like it.

But it was his worst football season not because of the injuries, or his sub-par play, or that the Bickering Bills spent most of 1989 fighting with each other, or that Buffalo lost in the wild-card round of the AFC playoffs to the Cleveland Browns. Bennett's worst season came when, for the first time in his life, people questioned his heart, questioned whether he was really trying his best, and that unacceptable and untrue characterization sliced deep into his soul.

"For the first time since I'd played football, negative things were being said about me," Bennett remembered. "From high school on, everything had always been good. Suddenly I'm turning on the TV and they're saying, 'Cornelius is loafing.'"

Lino Bennett never loafed a day in his life and neither did his son Cornelius, one of six children Lino and his loving wife Lillie raised on his

Cornelius Bennett, who wore No. 55 when he first came to Buffalo, celebrates one of his many Bills victories with Jim Kelly. **Courtesy of the Buffalo Bills**

steelworker's wage in Birmingham, Alabama. There was no way Cornelius could ever take a play off, because by doing so, he would be disrespecting his father and all that he stood for.

"By the end of that season, listening to the things that were said about me, I was ready to fight everybody, fight the world," Bennett said. "I was even thinking about quitting football because it was tough on me, tough on my marriage, tough on my family."

Of course, he did not quit. His father wouldn't have quit, so neither would Cornelius. Between the end of 1989 and the start of the 1990 season, Bennett worked harder than he ever had to make sure his body was 100 percent healthy and strong.

If ever there was anyone born to play football, it was Bennett. He came into this world weighing 11 pounds, four ounces, and announced his presence by kicking over a tray that was attached to his hospital crib, prompting the nurse to proclaim, "This boy is going to be a football player."

Was he ever. He starred at Ensley High in Birmingham, and as the top college prospect in the state he chose to stay at home and attend the University of Alabama. Bennett rushed for 1,099 yards and caught 12 touchdown passes as a senior tight end/running back combination, but when he arrived on campus, coach Ray Perkins had a surprise for him.

"Here I was, the best running back coming out of the South, ahead of Brent Fullwood and a couple other guys, and all of a sudden I get to college and Ray Perkins says, 'I want to try you at linebacker,'" Bennett recalled. "Thinking back on it, I think he tricked me into playing linebacker."

Perkins had been Lawrence Taylor's first NFL coach with the New York Giants before leaving Gotham to take over for the retired Bear Bryant at Alabama. One look at Bennett and Perkins proclaimed that he was "the next Lawrence Taylor."

"I wasn't too far off," Perkins said. "I saw some of the same things in him that I saw in Lawrence."

During his time at Alabama Bennett made 287 tackles, 42 for lost yardage including 16 sacks. As a senior, he became the first linebacker to win the Lombardi Trophy, normally given to the best lineman in the nation, and on draft day 1987, Bennett was the second overall choice by the Indianapolis Colts after Tampa Bay picked Heisman Trophy winner Vinny Testaverde.

He never played a down in Indianapolis, though. His agent and Colts president Jim Irsay could not reach a contract agreement and Bennett held out, vowing to sit the entire year if need be.

That wasn't necessary. The Bills, Colts and Los Angeles Rams worked out an elaborate blockbuster trade, and when the dust settled, Bennett landed in Buffalo, Eric Dickerson moved from Los Angeles to Indianapolis, and the Rams received from Buffalo running back Greg Bell and a bevy of draft picks including first-rounders in 1988 and 1989.

"He told me the day that he signed that we were going to become winners," said Buffalo's general manager at the time, Bill Polian. "He kept his word."

GAME DAY SETTING

Since taking over as general manager in 1985 Polian had made tangible progress on the rebuilding of the Buffalo franchise after it had sunk to the depths of the NFL with back-to-back 2-14 seasons.

Every one of his moves played a part in transforming the Bills from the laughingstock of the mid-1980s to the AFC's dominant team in the late 80s and early 90s. However, if you ask Polian which transaction in particular was the most important, his answer is unequivocal.

"In a narrow context, specifically answering the question, it was the trade for Cornelius," he said. "We felt that trade gave us an opportunity to be a really good defense."

Following a stunning come-from-behind victory over the Dolphins in the first game after the end of the NFL players strike, the Bills were 3-3 and there was excitement in the autumn air, a feeling that had been absent in Buffalo since 1981. And then the electricity really began to flow in the days

Cornelius Bennett, shown sacking Drew Bledsoe (later a Bills quarterback), was one of the game's finest linebackers during his days in Buffalo. **Courtesy of the Buffalo Bills**

following the Miami game when word began to leak that the Colts were entertaining trade offers for their unsigned first-round pick, Bennett.

It had become apparent Bennett was never going to play in Indianapolis, so the Colts put him on the trading block and Polian and Marv Levy drooled at the prospect of obtaining him. In Buffalo's 3-4 defense, Bruce Smith needed another big-time pass rusher coming from the other side so that teams didn't continually slide their protections his way. Also, Shane Conlan was better suited to playing inside linebacker, but because the Bills were thin outside, the rookie was forced to play out of position. Getting Bennett would allow Levy to shift Conlan inside.

"Cornelius allowed Shane and Bruce to operate at their maximum efficiency," said Polian. "And it allowed Cornelius to flourish as well. It didn't just impact one player, it impacted three."

After nearly a week of exhaustive negotiations, with Polian fending off overtures from Houston, Washington and Tampa Bay (where Bennett's old Alabama coach Perkins was now employed), the deal was consummated on Halloween night.

Trick or treat?

Bills defensive coordinator Walt Corey provided the answer when, just a few games into Bennett's Buffalo career, before the new outside linebacker even knew what he was doing in the defense, Corey was heard to say, "The guy is amazing."

Denver's John Elway was thinking the same thing when he saw the linebacker staring at him from across the line of scrimmage when Bennett made his NFL debut.

THE GAME

November 8, 1987
BILLS 21, BRONCOS 14

Bennett's head was spinning on the Monday following Buffalo's loss to Washington. In a whirlwind week of trade talks, contract negotiations, and finally shuffling off to Buffalo, Cornelius faced his toughest challenge yet—restarting a football career that had lain stagnant for almost 10 months.

With all that behind him, now he had to get down to the business of meeting his new teammates and coaches and learning how to play the Bills' defense.

"I had a meeting with Walt Corey and we sat down and went over the defense, but it was in one ear and out the other," Bennett recalled. "I went down to the locker room and when I got off the elevator Darryl Talley happened to see me with the playbook and Darryl pulled me aside and told me to put the playbook in the bottom of my locker. He said, 'Whatever you need to know, I'll teach you.' So I had a great tutor and mentor in Darryl."

It was uncertain how the Bills planned to use Bennett in his first NFL game, the game of his life, which happened to be against Elway and the reigning AFC champion Denver Broncos. The consensus was that Bennett would not start but that he would see spot duty, and that proved correct.

However, things got a little skewed thereafter. The assumption was that even when Bennett was on the field he wouldn't be able to contribute much to Buffalo's defensive effort. After all, he was a rookie playing in his first NFL game without the benefit of mini-camp and training camp practices, with almost no knowledge of the defense, and with a body that hadn't endured live football contact since the previous January when he played his final college game in the Senior Bowl.

Bennett blew that notion to smithereens on his very first play.

"The first time I ran onto the field I got a pressure on Elway and knocked him down," Bennett recalled, smiling at the thought. "I remember thinking to myself, 'I'm finally here.'"

It happened late in the first quarter on Buffalo's second defensive series. The Denver defense had just recovered a fumble by Jamie Mueller at the Broncos 20 and when a pair of runs left Denver in a third-and-six, Bennett was sent onto the field with one mission: Get Elway.

"I knew the basic defense, but they pretty much put me out there and said, 'Go get the quarterback, go get the man with the ball,'" said Bennett.

So that's what he did. Elway took a shotgun snap and Bennett, unburdened by any responsibilities in pass coverage or run support, came smashing through the Bronco line and was on Elway almost as soon as he caught the ball. Ever the escape artist, Elway managed to throw the ball away to avoid the sack, but Denver was forced to punt. Bennett had done his job.

The crowd roared its approval, and the Bills mobbed Bennett when he came to the sidelines.

"After all the holdout stuff I went through, to finally fulfill a dream come true by playing in the NFL, and then I was playing against John Elway; and my very first play the fans were crazy, and I was nervous as all get-out and to be able to come out and rush him into an incompletion was really something," Bennett said. "That's a memory I think about all the time."

In fact, that play means so much to Bennett that he can barely remember what happened in the final minute of the game when he recorded the first sack of his career, nailing Elway for an eight-yard loss.

"I think I started out on the right side coming off the offensive left side," Bennett said, unable to recall specifics or that it was a play that helped the Bills seal a 21-14 victory, which officially stamped them as playoff contenders.

"I can't imagine somebody with three days' practice, 10 months off from football, having the impact he had," Levy said after the game.

Energized by Bennett's debut and the fact that they had a gusty 30 mph wind at their back in the second quarter, the Bills shook off a shaky start that included turnovers on their first two possessions and turned a scoreless game into a veritable rout with 18 unanswered points.

After Bennett's near sack of Elway forced Denver to punt, the Bills took over at their own 36 and 10 plays later were in the end zone when Jim Kelly hit Andre Reed for a nine-yard touchdown. Later in the quarter, Robb Riddick blocked a Denver punt through the end zone for a safety, then he scored on a one-yard run to cap a 75-yard drive. Steve Tasker then blocked a second Denver punt out of the end zone on the final play of the first half for an 18-0 Buffalo lead, making this one of only 18 games in NFL history where two or more safeties were recorded.

The lead went to 21-0, but Elway put two touchdowns on the board and when Tasker fumbled the kickoff after the second TD and Marc Munford recovered for the Broncos at the Buffalo 11 with 5:39 left to play, Bennett's coming out party was in danger of being spoiled. However, on second-and-goal from the seven Bruce Smith jarred the ball away from Sammy Winder and Nate Odomes recovered the fumble, averting a potential disaster.

When the Buffalo offense, which had managed just one first down in its previous four possessions, was able to churn out three and burn all but 49 seconds off the game clock, the Bills were safe.

Well, check that. Elway still had one more chance, though he needed to go 80 yards against a gale in less than a minute with no timeouts. It would have taken a miracle, and the Bills weren't in the miracle business just yet. Bennett blew into the backfield to sack Elway, and then safety Dwight Drane recovered a fumble by Denver tight end Clarence Kay who was attempting to lateral on a last-ditch gadget play.

Game over, career underway, and an official Elway endorsement after the game told Bennett: "Welcome to the NFL."

SINCE THE GAME

Bennett became an All-Pro in 1988, and after that rough patch in 1989, he earned Pro Bowl invitations from 1990 through 1993 as a mainstay on the Buffalo team that won an unprecedented four straight AFC championships.

"The reaction when we got Cornelius was phenomenal," said Andre Reed. "That pushed us to the forefront. That was the biggest trade in the league in many years, it was a blockbuster trade, and what Cornelius did that first game when we played the Broncos and he was in Elway's face all the time, which was great for the fans. We knew getting him in Buffalo, that kind of pushed us over the edge. He was the missing piece of the puzzle for our defense."

Said Bennett: "You see things on ESPN and they talk about big trades, and that one is in the top 10 of all time, so that makes me feel good that my name is associated with it. And then to come in and out of all the people and draft picks that were traded, our team had the most success out of any of those teams, so that makes me feel pretty good.

"I knew that if other guys had the same attitude I had as far as winning was concerned, we were going to be a winner. Growing up I was always the leader and the bell cow as many of my old coaches would say. I knew guys would follow me, and if I came to this team and guys were like me, we were going to be a winner."

CHAPTER TWELVE

Fred Smerlas

Position: Nose tackle
Number: 76
Years with Bills: 1979-89
Other teams: 49ers (1990), Patriots (1991-92)
College: Boston College
Born: April 8, 1957
Hometown: Waltham, Massachusetts
Current residence: Waltham, Massachusetts
Current occupation: CEO of All-Pro Productions; radio and television broadcaster

Fred became a member of the Bills Wall of Fame in 2001…was selected to play in five Pro Bowls and was a seven-time choice for all-AFC…earned the Ralph C. Wilson Distinguished Service Award in 1999…played in 162 games with the Bills including a streak of 156 consecutive starts which began midway through his 1979 rookie season…finished his Buffalo career with 595 tackles, 29.5 sacks, 10 fumble recoveries, and two interceptions.

THIS IS FRED SMERLAS

It was during his one year playing for the San Francisco 49ers, and later the two years he played for his hometown New England Patriots, that Fred Smerlas came to realize just how much being a member of the Buffalo Bills meant to him.

"It was never the same for me after I left, because in my heart I wasn't a San Francisco 49er or a New England Patriot; I was a Buffalo Bill," Smerlas said. "When I was in San Fran I used to wear a Bills t-shirt under my uniform. Guys couldn't understand it, but I told them if you had experienced what I experienced in Buffalo, you'd understand.

"And I remember in New England, I'm wearing the same t-shirt and I take my shoulder pads off and the guy standing next to me says, 'No matter what uniform you put on, you'll still be a Buffalo Bill underneath.' That was kind of fitting."

Sometimes masked by his cartoon-like personality—think Fred Flintstone with a bushy moustache and muscles—and his ability to make people laugh is the fact that Smerlas is one of the all-time great Bills.

His name is affixed to the Wall of Fame at Ralph Wilson Stadium not because of all those great quotes he used to provide, or all those chicken wings he used to eat, but because he was the pre-eminent player at his position for nearly a decade, good enough to be voted to five Pro Bowls.

Smerlas left Buffalo following the 1989 season and signed with the 49ers as a Plan B free agent, and a couple years later Shane Conlan paid him the ultimate compliment when he told him, "I never appreciated you until you were gone, because no one used to hit me."

Said Shane Nelson: "Jimmy Haslett and I got much of the credit [when they and Smerlas formed the Bermuda Triangle during the early 1980s] because we were piling up tackles, but it was Fred who made it all happen. He was an immovable force. He made our jobs a whole lot easier."

Smerlas was born to be a nose tackle, though it took a while for that talent to shine through. He weighed 10 pounds when he came crashing out of his mother's womb, but for much of his childhood years his size did not translate into athletic prowess.

"I used to play with the girls, I was a little fat guy," Smerlas said. "I didn't like sports. I played chess, I played Stratego, I played with my chemistry set, and I played dollhouses with my little girlfriends. I was the last kid picked for everything. I didn't even watch sports. I hated sports."

But Smerlas never backed down from anybody and that trait served him well growing up in Waltham, Massachusetts.

"Our neighborhood looked like Wally Cleaver's neighborhood, but it had all Eddie Haskells in it," he said. "It was a mill town and the families who lived there had moved there from tougher areas. There were like 50 kids

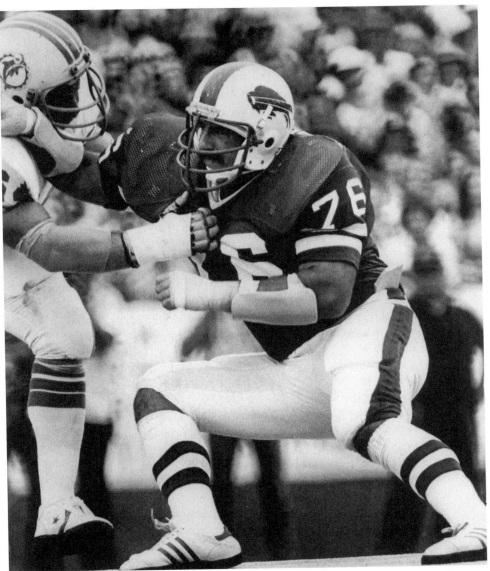

He may have been a comedian off the field, but on the field Fred Smerlas was all business, earning five Pro Bowl invitations. **Courtesy of Robert L. Smith (Orchard Park, NY)**

who were the same age, and all the kids were tough. I always got along because I never cried if I got beat up. They respected me because I didn't quit."

Smerlas didn't play football until he started ninth grade at Waltham High. "All my buddies went out for football, and we had these nutty coaches and I said, 'This sucks,' and I wanted to quit, but after school the guys would say, 'Don't quit, we're all here, afterward we'll go out and party.' I enjoyed the camaraderie, but football sucked."

He may not have liked the game, but he began to dominate it.

By the time he was a junior he had grown to six foot two and weighed 230 burly pounds, and had become a star on the wrestling team. During his last two years in high school, Smerlas earned All-America honors in both football and wrestling, he won all 60 of his wrestling matches to win a pair of state heavyweight championships, and he was an all-state shot putter in track and field.

"I started lifting weights so that I could defend myself, and to get girls," he said. "As I hit puberty everything just kind of came together. I was uncoordinated, but then I gained 100 pounds in high school and started doing well in sports and all of a sudden I started getting letters [from college recruiters] and I was like, 'Man, someone's going to pay for me to go to school.'"

Boston College, located five miles from his home, wound up footing the bill and Smerlas paid dividends as he became one of the Eagles' best players, though his days on Chestnut Hill ended poorly as the Eagles suffered through a miserable 0-11 season in 1978.

However, Smerlas cemented his pro football future by the way he played that year. The Bills' scouting director, Norm Pollom, was hugely impressed with the way Smerlas persevered and he said, "I've never seen a guy play better on a bad team. When a guy plays like that on a poor team, you've got someone you know is going to be there all the time."

"We call it the perfect season up here, and I was one of the captains of the perfect season," Smerlas recalled with a laugh. "It's a team sport, but you have to take pride in what you do first and don't worry about the other guys around you. So when I was in the game, my focus was killing the guy in front of me. Playing team defense, but playing the best I can within the game and kill the guy in front of me. That helped me when I got into the pros because we had a couple 2-14 seasons, and when things weren't going well I was able to get into my world and focus on what I had to do."

The Bills chose linebacker Tom Cousineau (who never signed with the Bills) and wide receiver Jerry Butler in the first round of the 1979 draft, then were flip-flopping between Mark Gastineau and Smerlas in the second round with the No. 32 overall pick. They opted for Smerlas and never regretted the decision. Gastineau was briefly one of the game's best pass rushers, but his star faded quickly, while Smerlas gave the Bills 11 productive and consistent years.

Smerlas started slowly in 1979 but worked himself into the starting lineup by mid-season, and by the time he bolted Buffalo after 1989 he had started in 155 consecutive games including the playoffs. He played in four straight Pro Bowls between 1980 and '83 as the Bills won one AFC East title, then put those perseverance skills to good use when the team hit rock bottom in the mid-'80s.

Sadly, Smerlas missed Buffalo's joyous ride to four straight AFC championships. After bleeding Buffalo red, white and blue for so long, he was told by Marv Levy at the end of the '89 season that his playing time was going to be cut because Levy wanted to play his defensive linemen in waves and Jeff Wright needed time at nose tackle. Smerlas was vehemently opposed and it was mutually decided that Smerlas should seek work elsewhere. He was left unprotected in Plan B free agency and signed with the defending Super Bowl champion 49ers.

Smerlas was gone in body, but never in spirit, and even though he now lives back in his native Waltham, his ties to Buffalo haven't severed and he still considers Western New York his second home.

"God made me a 300-pound, strong Greek man so I can kick ass on the field; he gave me the gift of gab so I could BS a beautiful girl [his wife Kris] to marry me; and he gave me the Buffalo Bills fans who will always be a part of my family," he said the day he was inducted into the Bills' Wall of Fame.

GAME DAY SETTING

Confidence was brimming during the 1988 training camp for the Bills. Marv Levy and his staff were firmly entrenched and quarterback Jim Kelly was going into his third year in the league and seemed ready to explode with his touchdown partner, wide receiver Andre Reed. Bruce Smith was on the brink of becoming the league's next great defensive player, the trade for Cornelius Bennett had injected life into the defense, and a rookie running back named Thurman Thomas was expected to do the same for the offense.

"In '87 we were starting to play pretty well, and going into '88 we had the right mesh of everything," Smerlas said. "We had the talent, we had the intensity, and most of all we had the camaraderie."

The Bills won their opener at home against a Minnesota team that many were picking to represent the NFC in the Super Bowl. Then came victories over Miami, New England, and Pittsburgh. The Bills were 4-0 for the first time since 1980 and though they had outscored those opponents by just 16 points combined, they had done what no one thought was possible—go 4-0 without Smith who had been suspended for violating the league's substance abuse policy.

Although the Bills lost to the Bears when Smith returned in Week 5, it turned out to be a small bump in the road. The Bills reeled off another six consecutive victories, including a pair of Monday night road blowouts, 37-14 over the Jets and 31-6 over the hated Dolphins, and now the Jets were coming into Orchard Park. If the Bills could extend their winning streak to seven they would clinch just their second AFC East division title, and Western New York was aflame all week in anticipation.

But during practice the Bills remained focused. New York would be playing without starting quarterback Ken O'Brien, who would be replaced by Pat Ryan, and the Jets had hardly provided a fight in the game at the

During his 11 years in Buffalo, Fred Smerlas became the preeminent nose tackle in the NFL. **Courtesy of the Buffalo Bills**

Meadowlands just over a month earlier. Still, with a 5-5-1 record, New York was in playoff contention and actually needed the game much more than Buffalo.

"Everyone thought it would merely be an extension of our previous weekend at the beach," Smerlas said of the fans and media. "But the Jets were determined not to let us do any celebrating at their expense."

Ultimately, the mother of all celebrations took place that day, but as the Bills expected, it took every ounce of energy and talent they could muster to get that party started.

THE GAME
November 20, 1988
BILLS 9, JETS 6 (OT)

Fandemonium: There is no such word in the English language, or any other language for that matter. Unless, that is, you happen to be a fan of the Bills.

Fandemonium is a slang term unique to Buffalo, coined by that renowned wordsmith, Darryl Talley, on a wet, raw, misty-aired and unforgettable day when the Bills clinched the first of the six AFC East titles they would win over the next eight years.

Fandemonium. From the English words "fan" and "pandemonium," put into context this way by Talley: "What do they call it, pandemonium? This was *fandemonium*."

It was genius, really, because conventional language could not describe the scene at Rich Stadium when Scott Norwood kicked a 30-yard field goal to give the Bills a 9-6 overtime victory over the New York Jets.

Within seconds of the ball plunging into the netting behind the tunnel-end goal post, a new word in the Western New York lexicon was born as Bills fans—eager to eradicate the memory of back-to-back 2-14 seasons in 1984 and 1985—could not contain their elation. They poured out of the stands until not one square foot of artificial turf was visible to celebrate this momentous victory.

"It was an unbelievable sight, an indescribable feeling," said Smerlas, who helped create that scene by blocking a 40-yard field goal attempt by New York's Pat Leahy with 19 seconds left in regulation, forcing the overtime that Norwood ended moments later. "That day will forever occupy a special place in my heart. That was definitely a memorable game. It was a big game, the game that kind of put us back on the map because we had been down for quite a while."

Not since 1981 had Buffalo competed in a playoff game, and in the interim, some of the worst football in Bills history had been played. Now the Bills had punched their ticket to the postseason, and it was easy to understand why Smerlas picked this as the game of his life.

"It was kind of like a dream at first, because we still had to go win the game," he said recalling his block of Leahy's field goal. "The adrenaline started to rush, guys were jumping up and down and doing cartwheels and the crowd's going crazy and then we got off the field and realized the game wasn't over. Then we went down, Norwood kicked the field goal, and we looked at each other and said, 'We finally got here.' It had been a climb."

Only a nose tackle could love a game like this. Defenses ruled the cold, damp day as neither Jim Kelly nor New York's Pat Ryan could get anything working on offense.

Leahy and Norwood traded two field goals apiece, and then midway through the fourth quarter the Jets were given the opportunity to delay Buffalo's celebration at least another week. One play after Kelly had completed a 35-yard pass to tight end Pete Metzelaars, putting the ball on the New York 25 with 4:30 to play, Thurman Thomas fumbled, and Scott Mersereau recovered for the Jets at the 30.

The Jets almost gave it right back when Talley forced Freeman McNeil to fumble, but New York's Billy Griggs fell on the loose ball, and from there Ryan pieced together a well-executed drive that pushed all the way to the Buffalo 23 where Bruce Smith stopped McNeil on a third-down play just shy of the first-down marker.

Out came Leahy with a chance to spoil the fun. Only 25 seconds showed on the clock and the ball was to be spotted at the Buffalo 30 for a 40-yard attempt. Leahy had made 47 of his previous 49 attempts from 40 yards or closer including the two in this game, but Smerlas had a feeling Leahy was due to miss.

"We looked at it on film and there were gaps that we could get in because they weren't closing down real tight," he said. "I just missed the one before by an inch, so I figured I could get it if I got a good enough jump on the ball. If we missed and go offsides, so what. You give him five more yards, big deal, he hadn't missed from there anyway. I was going on flinch. I saw the center tighten up on the ball and went through clean. I caught his arm as he snapped the ball and twisted through the gap and straightened up and leaped as high as I could leap, which wasn't very high at all and I remember just getting my fat fingers on it."

Count center Kent Hull among those who thought the game was over.

"I couldn't bear to watch," he said. "It looked like a chip shot and I figured no way he was going to miss. Freddie looked like Michael Jordan on that one. When he made that block, I knew there was no way we were going to lose."

Hull was right. The Jets won the coin toss to start overtime, but on the second play from scrimmage, Buffalo cornerback Derrick Burroughs stripped fullback Roger Vick of the ball and Cornelius Bennett recovered at the Jets 32.

With the crowd ready to explode, sensing a magical moment, Robb Riddick ran four consecutive times to move the ball to the 12, and on third-and-two, Marv Levy sent Norwood into the game to attempt the winning field goal. Norwood, who had already won three games earlier in the season with late field goals, calmly center-cut the 30-yarder, and then there was *fandemonium*.

"The thing about Buffalo—and I played in other cities—it's a small town where they kind of live your life," said Smerlas. "You see them when you go out to the store and you're part of the community. When they ran on the field that day it was like all your buddies coming over for a drinking party. The fans are jumping on us, we're hugging everybody, and it was like a community on the field. A lot of times people run on the field and you think something bad is going to happen, because they're going to go nuts. But Buffalo's not like New York City or some of these other places where there's a lot of assholes. These people come to the game, pay their hard-earned money, and they share in the pain and the ecstasy. Coming out of the Hank Bullough era and living through it, then standing there in the tunnel and looking out onto the field with 80,000 people chanting, 'Fred-die, Fred-die,' I had tears coming down my cheeks."

SINCE THE GAME

In 1989, the Bills won another AFC East title but lost in the first round at Cleveland in the final game Smerlas would play as a Bill. He wrapped up his career playing for the 49ers and Patriots, then retired following the 1992 season.

"I couldn't get a job coming out of football because my resume read, 'Ran into people with his head' and that doesn't qualify you for much," he said with his typical humor.

However, he ultimately found the perfect job. Using his gift of gab, he became a staple in the Boston-area media. He does postgame shows after Patriots games for radio station WEEI as well as for the ABC television affiliate in Boston. He owns and produces a football show on FoxNet New England that he co-hosts, which is the highest-rated product on the network.

He is also CEO of All-Pro Productions, a company he founded that does promotional and fund-raising projects year-round. At Patriots home games, the company has a large tent near Gillette Stadium and it provides corporations with limousine service, live entertainment, food and drinks, before and after the games.

"I'm a pirate. I'm self-employed, and things have gone well," he said.

CHAPTER THIRTEEN

Don Beebe

Position: Wide receiver
Number: 82
Years with Bills: 1989-94
Other teams: Panthers (1995), Packers (1996-97)
College: Chadron (Nebraska) State
Born: December 18, 1964
Birthplace: Aurora, Illinois
Current residence: Aurora, Illinois
Current occupation: High school football coach; owns speed-training business called House of Speed

Don finished his career with 219 receptions for 3,416 yards and 23 TDs…his four-touchdown game against Pittsburgh in 1991 tied the Bills' record for most TD receptions in a game…after losing four Super Bowls with the Bills, he finally won a Super Bowl ring playing for the Packers in 1996…he also lost a Super Bowl in 1997 with the Packers, giving him a record six appearances in the game.

THIS IS DON BEEBE

The mail came pouring in for months, so fast and furious that Don Beebe could barely keep up with it.

Parents wrote to him saying they hoped their children would grow up to be just like him. Coaches wrote to him saying he represented all that was good about sports. Teachers wrote to him saying he had taught their students a lesson they'd been trying unsuccessfully to drive home.

The lesson? That you never quit, you never give up, you keep playing until the final whistle sounds, no matter how dire the situation.

"The letters—at first just the volume of letters—was unbelievable," Beebe said. "The ones that touched me the most were from the fathers."

Such as this one that Beebe reprinted in his book *More Than a Ring*, which he wrote after he had finally won a Super Bowl ring in 1996 playing for the Green Bay Packers.

"I've never been able to reach my son," the note began. *"We've never had a great relationship. Then I see this play where you don't give up. I show my son this play and say, 'This is how you act in sports and in life.' Our relationship changed because of it. You'll never understand how much your action meant to a lot of people. Thank you."*

Beebe admits to crying as he read that letter. And it was that letter, and hundreds more just like it, that made Beebe realize how important his ultimate act of hustle had been.

Dallas defensive lineman Leon Lett was running freely to the end zone after recovering a Bills' fumble in the fourth quarter of the Buffalo nightmare that was Super Bowl XXVII. At the time the score was 52-17, and just about every member of the embarrassed Buffalo team was willing the clock to tick faster so the horror would end and they could get out of the Rose Bowl.

Everyone, that is, besides Beebe. So when he saw Dallas's Jim Jeffcoat knock the ball from quarterback Frank Reich's grasp and Lett pick it up at the Cowboys' 35-yard line and start chugging the other way with Buffalo's Super Bowl-record ninth turnover, Beebe did what he had always done: Play 100 percent for 60 minutes.

"I was running a fly pattern down the left sideline," Beebe explained. "When I turned and looked, I saw Frank scrambling a bit. I was at least 40 yards from Frank and I started working my way back. Then Frank fumbled. When I saw him [Lett] pick up the ball, I started sprinting."

In Beebe's mind, despite the huge head start he was spotting Lett, running down the big fella wasn't the issue. Once he got there, Beebe wasn't quite sure what he was going to do. "With about 20 yards left I was thinking, 'How am I going to do this?' I'm thinking, 'This guy is huge.' To tell you the truth I was going to jump on his back."

Steve Tasker pats Don Beebe on the head after Beebe scored the first touchdown of his career in a game against Houston. **Courtesy of the Buffalo Bills**

He didn't have to. As Lett reached the 10-yard-line, unaware that Beebe was hot on his tail, and thinking he had a sure touchdown, he decided to showboat for the worldwide audience and held the ball out with his right hand.

"Unfortunately for him, he put it out there and gave me an opportunity to slap it away," said Beebe, who pulled off that maneuver and sent the ball careening out of the end zone, preventing not only a Dallas touchdown but giving possession of the ball back to the Bills.

At first, as the crowd of nearly 100,000 stood there, stunned by what had just happened, Beebe didn't even think about what he had done. He ripped off his helmet in anger and walked back to the Buffalo bench, aggravated by the Bills' continued colossal failure.

"What was there to celebrate?" he said. "We were getting beaten badly."

But he would soon come to understand that while his play did nothing to affect the outcome of the game, the example he set changed countless lives for the better.

"The first time it meant anything to me was after the game," Beebe recalled. "I was sitting in front of my locker, and I was upset that we lost. But then the Bills' owner, Ralph Wilson, walked by my locker, shook my hand, looked me square in the face and said, 'Son, you showed me a lot today. That meant a lot to me, that a guy like you can represent the Buffalo Bills like that. Thank you.'"

GAME DAY SETTING

Don and Barb Beebe brought five children into this world, and the future NFL player of the bunch came right in the middle of older sisters Beth and Diane, and younger brothers Dave and Dan. It came as no surprise to anyone in his family that Don did what he did that day at the Rose Bowl, because from an early age he had a competitive streak that was second to none.

Whether it was fishing contests on the lake at the family's vacation home in Minnesota or a game of one-on-one basketball, Don was determined to win. He wouldn't settle for anything less. And he's no different today.

He used that determination to his advantage in his athletic career. At Kaneland High School in Sugar Grove, Illinois, he played basketball and football, and for a while, basketball was his sport of choice. However, his dad pointed out that there wasn't much need in college for five-foot-10 basketball players, so Don turned back to football and played well enough to earn a scholarship to Western Illinois.

So began an adventurous journey to the NFL. He lasted only a year at Western Illinois as he became disillusioned with the sport because of the militaristic style of coach Bruce Craddock. After not playing in the fall of 1983, he transferred to Aurora College in Illinois and played one year of basketball on the junior varsity team, then quit school altogether and went to work for his brother-in-law who owned an aluminum siding business.

After two years on a ladder he began to miss football, and dreams of playing in the NFL consumed his thoughts. He re-enrolled at Western Illinois, was improperly declared ineligible in 1986, which cost him a season, then played in 1987 and used his last year of NCAA eligibility to earn all-conference honors.

With just one year of college football on his resume, he was told it would be virtually impossible to get a scout from the NFL to notice him, but Western Illinois assistant coach Randy Ball had a potential solution. Ball alerted Beebe to the fact that NAIA schools had different eligibility rules than the NCAA and that he would still have two years left under their guidelines.

One year was all it took for Beebe to grab the NFL's attention. Beebe chose Chadron State in Nebraska, where former Western Illinois assistant

Brad Smith was the head coach, and he caught 49 passes for 906 yards and 13 touchdowns plus averaged 25 yards on kickoff returns. NFL scouts flocked to the tiny school in the northwest corner of the state, and Beebe blew them away with his blazing speed, often clocking 4.2 or 4.3 seconds in the 40-yard dash.

The Bills did not have a first- or second-round draft pick that year, having given both away to acquire linebacker Cornelius Bennett in a 1987 trade, so with their first selection, in the third round, No. 82 overall (which happened to be the number Beebe would wear), the Bills took Beebe.

"We did a lot of research on Don," said the Bills' general manager at the time, Bill Polian. "We knew Don was the kind of person we wanted on our football team."

Beebe made the team as the No. 4 receiver behind Andre Reed, Chris Burkett and Flip Johnson, and didn't even get on the field in Buffalo's first two games of 1989. However, Burkett was waived after engaging in a sideline argument with Kelly during a 28-14 Monday night loss to Denver and Burkett was released. Just like that Beebe was the No. 3 man who would be making his NFL debut at the Houston Astrodome in a game later that week against the Oilers.

And that day—during one of the wildest games in Bills history—Larry Felser wrote in the *Buffalo News* that Beebe "hit the football equivalent of a bases-loaded home run in his first at-bat."

THE GAME

September 24, 1989
BILLS 47, OILERS 41 (OT)

As Beebe trotted out to the right side of the formation to participate in just the second play of his NFL career, and Houston cornerback Cris Dishman crept up to the line of scrimmage to greet him, Beebe knew there was a very good possibility his life was about to change.

"We go to Houston and the first play I'm on the field in my career is a running play," Beebe recalled. "I go out there and it's Sunday afternoon, national television, everyone's watching on TV back home, and I'm out there against the Oilers and Cris Dishman is pressing me. He's right up in my face and he goes, 'Hey, white boy, I hear you can run. Let's see it, man.' But it's a running play, and I'm scared to death, so I just block him.

"We didn't get the first down, so we punt. Then on the next series it's third down again and Jim looks at me and says, 'Beebs, if Dishman is pressing you again, just take him deep. I don't care what kind of route you've got, just take him deep because I'm going to throw it to you.' Sure enough Dishman is pressing me and I got a great release on him and ran by him and it was a 63-yard bomb for a touchdown."

Beebe's nine-year career spent with Buffalo, Carolina and Green Bay was filled with many thrilling victories and heartbreaking defeats, but the game of his life was the first game he ever played, not only because his first career reception happened to go for a long touchdown, but because it was the culmination of a fascinating pilgrimage to professional football.

"That changed everything for us," Steve Tasker said of Beebe's emergence that day in Houston. "All of a sudden teams realized they had to cover us deep. Now we had someone who could really go. We had a Hall of Famer in James Lofton [who would join the team just two days after the Oilers game] on one side, we had Andre, who may be the best slot receiver in the history of the game, and now we had Beebe, who could just fly. The whole dynamic of the offense changed. They couldn't sit on the short routes, it was a matchup nightmare."

It was certainly a nightmare for Dishman, a future Pro Bowl performer who, at the time, was a speedy cornerback in his second year in the league.

"He was talking some trash saying, 'You can't run, I can stay with you,' and it was all in fun," said Beebe. "But then the next time I'm out there, he gets in my face, and he gets in that squat position and he says, 'Dang, I guess the white boy can run.' It's kind of funny throughout the rest of our careers, whenever we would play against each other, he would kid me about that."

Beebe's touchdown helped Buffalo nip the Oilers 47-41 in overtime for its first victory ever at the Astrodome in what remains the highest-scoring regular-season game the Bills have ever played.

"It was an unbelievable game," said Beebe. "It was one of the great games in Bills' history. I don't know what it was for the Oilers."

It was a disaster, that's what it was for the Oilers.

The Bills turned a pair of interceptions off Warren Moon into two scores, and on the final play of the first half Darryl Talley blocked a field goal and Mark Kelso scooped the bouncing ball off the turf and raced 77 yards for a touchdown that sent Buffalo flying into the intermission ahead 20-10.

Beebe's NFL debut had come late in the first half when he blocked on the failed third-down run, and his second play came on Buffalo's first possession of the third quarter.

"It was the first pass to ever come my way," he said. "I looked back and it looked like it was a punt because Jim had thrown it so high. I lost it in the lights at one point and then I caught it. If you watch the video I got it one-handed and brought it in and it was one of the best catches I ever made. It looked easy, but it really wasn't."

When Beebe returned to the sideline clutching the ball that not only represented his first NFL reception but his first NFL touchdown, he broke down in a sea of tears.

"I remember after I scored I didn't know what to do, so I kind of skipped and I got made fun of by Andre," Beebe said with a laugh. "I'm walking over to the bench and I sit down and I think, geez, I know all my family is going nuts in the house watching this game, watching what their brother and their son has just done, and I couldn't hold back the tears. I was just crying on the sidelines, full of emotion over what just happened in my life."

As for the game, things got a little crazy when the Bills failed to protect their 27-10 lead. Dishman exacted a measure of revenge when he scooped up a punt that was blocked by Bubba McDowell, then ran seven yards for a touchdown to cut the Oilers' deficit to 27-24.

One play after the ensuing kickoff, on the first play of the fourth quarter, Reed caught a short comeback pass from Kelly and sprinted 78 yards for a touchdown. It looked as if the Bills were back in control.

Not quite. Moon fired a 26-yard touchdown pass to Ernest Givins, and after Steve Brown picked off a Kelly pass and returned it 41 yards to the Buffalo seven, Lorenzo White plowed into the end zone from the one, and the Oilers were on top 38-34 with 4:40 remaining.

Kelly, who had called the Astrodome his home for two years when he played for the Houston Gamblers in the U.S. Football League, strapped on his holster and went back to gunslinging. He completed four straight passes to advance the ball to the Oilers 20, and after a sack forced him into a third-and-16, he found Thurman Thomas all alone on the right sideline for a 26-yard touchdown that put the Bills into the lead, 41-38, with 1:52 to go.

Again it wasn't enough as Moon engineered a march that ended with Tony Zendejas kicking a tying 52-yard field goal with three seconds remaining to force overtime.

Houston won the coin toss to start the extra period and it had a chance to win, but Zendejas missed wide left from 37 yards. Kelly took the field and capped off what was to that point his greatest NFL passing yardage day (363 yards) by throwing his fifth touchdown of the game, a 28-yard strike to Reed that ended the game.

"To be honest, the only other play I remember in that game—I don't remember anything else—was Andre catching a hitch and taking it to the house to win the game in overtime," said Beebe.

SINCE THE GAME

When Beebe joined the Packers in 1996 after one unproductive and disheartening season with the expansion Carolina Panthers, he knew he was joining a talented team with the potential to win the NFC.

After being on the losing side in four Super Bowls, he said, "All I want to do is go to the Super Bowl and win. I want to know what that feels like. If it's carrying water to Reggie White when he's tired, I'll do that."

One of the fastest men to ever wear a Bills uniform, Don Beebe was a member of six teams that advanced to the Super Bowl, appearing four times—including three with Buffalo. **Courtesy of the Buffalo Bills**

Beebe did much more. He caught 39 passes, four for touchdowns, and he led the Packers with a 17.9-yard average per reception. In a memorable Monday night game in October against San Francisco he caught 11 passes for 220 yards, the third highest receiving yardage output in the Packers' long and illustrious history.

Green Bay rolled through the regular season with a 13-3 record, then blew out the 49ers in the divisional playoff and Beebe's former Carolina team in the NFC Championship. The Packers, winners of the first two Super Bowls, were going back to the big dance for the first time in 29 years, and Beebe was joining them for the ride.

Beebe did not catch a pass in Super Bowl XXXI, and his role had actually been rather minimal. But when Brett Favre took a knee to wrap up Green Bay's 35-21 victory over New England at the New Orleans Superdome, Beebe was on the field, and as soon as Favre stood up, Beebe came over and asked above the roaring Packer fans partying in the Bayou, "Can I have the game ball?" Favre, recognizing Beebe's long wait for the elusive Super Bowl ring, said, "You bet. You deserve it," and he flipped it to him.

Beebe retired quietly following the 1997 season and he made a smooth transition into his post-football life as he started a business called House of Speed, based in his hometown of Sugar Grove, Illinois, where he trains athletes using his patented techniques to improve speed, balance and mental toughness.

In 2004, he became a high school football coach, taking over the program at Aurora Christian.

"When kids get a chance to stand next to him and see a guy like Don who had a great career as a pro because he was smart, fast and tough, that gives them a lot of hope," said Beebe's old Buffalo pal, Steve Tasker. "Coaching high school is perfectly suited for him. The kids will learn a lot."

CHAPTER FOURTEEN

Darryl Talley

Position: Linebacker
Number: 56
Years with Bills: 1983-94
Other teams: Falcons (1995), Vikings (1996)
College: West Virginia
Born: July 10, 1960
Birthplace: Cleveland, Ohio
Current residence: Windermere, Florida
Current occupation: Owner—Sentry Barricade

Darryl ranks second on the Bills' all-time tackle list with 1,137. Also had 38.5 sacks, 11 interceptions and 10 fumble recoveries...played in 16 playoff games with the Bills and recorded 124 tackles, 6.5 sacks and two interceptions...was selected to play in two Pro Bowls...was inducted into the Bills' Wall of Fame in 2003...played in 188 games as a Bill which ranks fifth all-time, and at one point he played in 181 straight games...is a member of the West Virginia University Hall of Fame and ranks second on Mountaineers' all-time tackle list with 484.

THIS IS DARRYL TALLEY

It really should have been the other way around, but no one thought of it. A couple of days after the Bills announced in April 1994 that they were going to have to release Darryl Talley because of salary cap restraints, Talley took out a full-page advertisement in *The Buffalo News* to thank the fans of Western New York for their support through the years. The ad read:

"In leaving Buffalo, I want to express my sincerest thanks to everyone who has made my 12 years here the most memorable time of my life. I will go away with only fond memories. To the people of Buffalo, thanks for making me feel like one of your own. On behalf of my family, thanks for the memories. It was my honor."

Anyone who spent their Sunday afternoons at Rich Stadium watching Talley—the ultimate warrior who never missed a game in his Bills career—would beg to differ. It was their honor watching No. 56 spill his blood and guts all over opposing quarterbacks, running backs, and wide receivers week after week after week.

The man took out a full-page newspaper ad to thank the fans. Name another modern-day athlete who would even think of the gesture. It was such a genuine display of class, but then again, one should consider the source. This man was the heart and soul of the Bills for much of his time in Buffalo. A man who truly understood what a privilege it was to play a game for a living. A man who worked regular shifts at a McDonald's restaurant one off season as part of his training to become a franchise owner when his playing days were over.

Ultimately, his post-football career path veered in a different direction and the McDonald's thing didn't work out. Football certainly worked out.

Though an undersized linebacker, Darryl starred on the football team at Shaw High School in Cleveland, and even then his willingness to play in pain was evident. He missed the first half of his senior year due to a broken ankle, but he was itching to get back on the field so he went up to his coach and proclaimed his readiness.

To further augment his case Talley said, "You want to know the difference in this football team? It's me."

He was right, but the coach rested him one more week and Shaw lost the game by a field goal. The following week Talley was back, Shaw upset the second-ranked team in the state, and his father claims Darryl earned his scholarship to West Virginia University that night.

"I was still skinny as a stop sign pole, but I could run and I could hit," Talley said.

Playing for the Mountaineers, he set the school's all-time record for career tackles with 484 (it has since been broken) including 135 in his senior season of 1982 when he was a consensus All-American. The Bills select-

Darryl Talley was considered the heart and soul of the Buffalo defense. **Courtesy of the Buffalo Bills**

ed him in the second round of the 1983 draft, the same draft that produced the future quarterback of the team, Jim Kelly.

Talley had enjoyed success at every level of football, but it took a while for him to flourish as a professional. He struggled to find his niche on a bad team his first two years, and then his progress was further impeded by the arrival in 1985 of defensive coordinator Hank Bullough who would also become the Bills' head coach for a little over a year.

When Bullough was fired midway through 1986 and Marv Levy was hired, Talley saw immediately that things were about to change, and his spirits continued to soar in 1987 when he began to learn new defensive coordinator Walt Corey's system.

"Walt took the chains off me," said Talley. "He just said, 'Go play football the way you can.' I could take off and run. They simplified the game."

Talley became as productive a linebacker as there was in the league, though no one outside of Buffalo seemed to notice. With so many big-name players on the team such as Kelly, Bruce Smith, Cornelius Bennett, Thurman Thomas, and Andre Reed, Talley quite naturally was overlooked.

Sometimes it bothered him, and one season he covered the nameplate above his locker with a piece of white tape with the name "Rodney" scribbled on it—a reference to Rodney Dangerfield, he of the 'no respect' mantra.

"We had a team full of stars and it's hard for everybody to shine," Talley said. "Somebody had to take a back seat. If you win and win big, there's always enough publicity to go around. Football's a team game. Individual accomplishments come from doing small things in the framework of a team. That's the way Darryl Talley played football. I've only been selfish about one thing: That's winning. I'm one of those people who want to win, and win at all costs. I don't like the idea of failing at anything."

Perhaps Talley's greatest contribution to the team, even beyond his 1,137 tackles and 38.5 sacks, was his leadership. There was no one—not even Kelly—who was more respected in the Buffalo locker room than Talley.

"You've got Bruce on one side of the ball, Jim on the other, and you have Thurman and Biscuit [Bennett] and Andre," said special teams ace Steve Tasker. "And Darryl was the only guy who felt comfortable enough to stand up and tell one of the superstars they were full of it, and to sit down and shut up. And they'd still love him afterward.

"He was a great player, we all loved him. The guy was just there, he was everybody's friend. He never overlooked anybody, he treated everybody the same. He was on your side, thick or thin, hell or high water. In a dark alley or the middle of Main Street, he had your back."

GAME DAY SETTING

Is it any wonder that Talley says, "I can remember 1990 like the back of my hand."

• It began the first weekend in January with a devastating playoff loss to the Cleveland Browns that ended Buffalo's tumultuous 1989 season when the team became known as the Bickering Bills.

• In the spring, Talley underwent operations to repair damage to his right knee and both elbows. All three procedures were performed on the same day. "When I think of him, I think of his toughness," said Talley's longtime teammate, Kent Hull.

• As training camp was about to begin in July, *Sport* magazine hit the newsstands with a story ranking linebackers in the NFL for all-around performance and value to a team. Talley's name—not Lawrence Taylor, not Mike Singletary, not Derrick Thomas, not his Buffalo teammate Cornelius Bennett—was at the very top. What made this so intriguing is that to this point in his career Talley had never been voted to a Pro Bowl, never been chosen for any all-star team and was going by the nickname "Rodney" because of his perceived lack of respect.

• He re-injured his knee in a preseason game and had to undergo another arthroscopic surgery three weeks before the start of the season, but made it back to play opening day and didn't miss a game all year.

"On Wednesday before the first game [trainer] Bud Carpenter was letting me do my running and I was still limping," Talley recalled. "Kelly was looking at me worrying that I wouldn't be able to play. I told him, 'If you're going to get underneath the center on Sunday, I'll be out there.' And there was nothing wrong with him."

• In a most satisfying return visit to his hometown of Cleveland, site of the Bills' playoff loss 10 months earlier, Talley intercepted two passes and returned one 60 yards for a touchdown to put the exclamation point on a 42-0 drubbing of the Browns.

• In the biggest game of the regular season, a 24-14 victory over Miami in which the Bills clinched their third straight AFC East division title, Talley was in on nine tackles and was named the AFC Defensive Player of the Week.

• After setting a team record with 13 regular-season victories, the Bills rolled through the AFC playoffs with victories over Miami and Los Angeles, and in the game of his life, that 51-3 demolition of the Raiders, Talley picked off two passes and returned one for a touchdown, helping to send the Bills to their first Super Bowl.

• Finally, during Super Bowl week it was announced that Talley would be making his first trip to Hawaii as Raiders coach Art Shell selected him as a "need" player for the Pro Bowl.

"Yeah, that was a pretty good year for me," Talley deadpanned before pointing out that the only thing lacking was a victory in Super Bowl XXV.

He set a new career-high with a team-leading 123 tackles and added four sacks, five QB pressures, two interceptions, a fumble recovery, and the type of leadership, on the field and off, which every team wishes it could have had.

"He wasn't thinking, 'I'm doing this to show what a leader I am,'" Marv Levy said. "His actions weren't necessarily subtle, but they were natural, infectious and truly genuine. And having it that way enhanced his leadership qualities. Young players tried to emulate the way he played. Darryl enjoyed the game. He didn't get flustered if the pendulum started swinging the other way. There was something about his presence when maybe you were experiencing some tough times that really was positive. He knew when to visit a player's locker, or give someone a non-embarrassing kick in the butt. And it meant something because he had the respect of the players because of how he played."

THE GAME

January 20, 1991
BILLS 51, RAIDERS 3

Four days after the Bills had whipped their archrivals from Miami in the AFC divisional playoff, and four days before they were to take on the Los Angeles Raiders in the AFC Championship Game, America entered the Persian Gulf War.

When Iraqi President Saddam Hussein ignored a United States-mandated deadline and refused to pull his troops out of Kuwait, President George H. Bush gave the go-ahead for American and Allied planes to unleash a massive bombing mission on targets in Iraq and occupied Kuwait.

All of a sudden, the outcome of a football game didn't matter quite as much.

Well, maybe not to those who weren't drawing a paycheck from the home office on One Bills Drive in Orchard Park, but to Talley and the rest of the Bills, beating the Raiders consumed their thoughts.

Of course, they were concerned for the troops overseas, the men and women who were fighting for our country and protecting our way of life. But NFL commissioner Paul Tagliabue said that until further notice, it was game on, and that meant only one thing to Talley.

"At that time we knew we were at war, but you're going into the biggest game of your life and we had to concentrate on that," Talley said. "We had to focus on that and only that. That was our job. Just like it was our troops' job to protect us in the war. We looked at it that way because we had to."

So the Bills prepared to meet the Raiders. They prepared as they had never prepared before. Then they went out and put forth a performance unmatched in team history, embarrassing Al Davis's proud Raiders, 51-3.

"I think it all started for our team back in 1987, the strike year," Talley said. "That year bonded us and made us better. I remember the last game that year, we were in Philadelphia, and I looked at Cornelius and said, 'We have a chance to be really good.' He looked at me and he said, 'You're right.'

"Then we had our coming-out party in 1988, made it to the AFC Championship Game and everyone was taken aback and saying, 'Where the hell did they come from?' In '89 we took a step back when we all had our attitude problems and we finally decided after that, 'We're not going to do this anymore. What's the purpose of being together if we're not a team, a unit?'

"We had a great nucleus of guys, but we were fighting amongst ourselves, and when it started becoming public knowledge, we knew we had to keep it in our house and check the egos at the door if we were going to do anything. It was just a matter of us deciding that we're good, we have an attitude about ourselves, we want to win and we will not quit."

By the time Jeff Jaeger kicked off to start the championship game, Hussein could have launched a counter-attack on Rich Stadium and the Bills wouldn't have heard the bombs, so focused were they on beating the Raiders. Only after the score reached 41-3 by halftime did they start to recognize what a truly special day it was.

"It was a super feeling to be out there," Talley said, remembering the sellout crowd waving American flags and Bills flags in an amalgam of patriotism and partisanship. "We weren't where we wanted to be yet, but to steal a line from Marv, 'Where else would you rather be than right here, right now?' It was a great day to be playing football in Western New York."

Not for the Raiders.

Moments after linebacker Shane Conlan had echoed a favorite Levy saying, bellowing in the Bills' pregame huddle, "When it's too tough for them, it's just right for us," the Bills took the opening kickoff and within 3:30 had a 7-0 lead as Jim Kelly hit James Lofton with a 13-yard touchdown pass.

Raiders quarterback Jay Schroeder responded by completing his first two passes for a total of 50 yards, but Talley knocked down his next attempt, then tackled Marcus Allen after a five-yard run to bring up third-and-five. Schroeder misfired again and Los Angeles settled for a 41-yard Jaeger field goal.

That was as close as the Raiders would get.

Four plays after the kickoff Thurman Thomas swept around right end for a 12-yard touchdown, and then late in the first quarter Talley made one of the biggest plays of his career and right then everyone knew the game was over.

Schroeder tried to throw a pass over the middle to Tim Brown, but when Bruce Smith pressured him, he had to release it a little early. Talley read the play perfectly, stepped in front to make the interception and then took off for the left corner of the end zone, crossing the goal line just before Brown could drag him down.

"[Assistant coach] Chuck Lester kept telling me to beware of the dig, a quick in," Talley explained. "They were notorious for it, throwing right behind the linebackers. So they set up in the formation, he was trying to

Darryl Talley (56), Bruce Smith (78), and Cornelius Bennett (97) joined forces to lead the defense during the Super Bowl years. **Courtesy of the Buffalo Bills**

throw to Tim Brown and I dropped back into coverage. I caught the ball and then I just started running toward the goal line. It seemed like it was going to take forever to get there."

The Bills tacked on three more touchdowns before the first half was complete, but Talley remembered there being no comfort in the laughable score. "I don't even think we thought about it. We were out there playing as hard as we could play on every play. Football is a game of how the ball bounces. If it bounced your way that day, you can be great. If it doesn't, it can turn on you, and we had seen that happen to us. We had been a part of that. We didn't care what the score was, we played every play like it was our last. Never relinquish the pressure, keep the heat on."

The second half was merely a formality, Talley contributing another interception that led to a field goal, and when the carnage was over, the Bills had tied the all-time scoring record for an AFC/AFL Championship Game and posted the third most lopsided victory in all playoff games. The 41 first-half points were a new postseason record, and Kelly's 73.9 completion per-centage and Buffalo's 30 first downs were AFC/AFL Championship Game marks.

Kelly passed for 300 yards and the Bills rushed for 202 (Thomas gain-ing 138) to set a new team postseason record of 502 total yards while the defense forced seven turnovers.

For Talley this game was the culmination of eight years of hard work.

"I thought about the bad years here," Talley said. "You'd go out in public and people would be snickering and laughing at you behind your back. I just tried to play as hard as I could during those times and I hoped eventually that better times would come."

SINCE THE GAME

Charles Dickens wrote "It was the best of times, it was the worst of times," and that certainly defined the plight of the Bills in the early 1990s.

Four consecutive years they won the AFC Championship Game, a run of unprecedented success. Four consecutive years they lost the Super Bowl, a run of unprecedented failure. The misery began the week after the rout of the Raiders when the Bills flew to Tampa for Super Bowl XXV and lost in heartbreaking fashion, 20-19, to the New York Giants.

"There are a lot of guys who played this game who never reached the Super Bowl," Talley said. "I was fortunate to have four bites of the apple, though I didn't eat the whole thing. It doesn't bother me that bad any more."

Maybe that's because Talley has moved on with his life, comfortable with his playing career and his accomplishments, and why not?

From 1990 through 1994, his last year in Buffalo, Talley led the Bills in tackles four times including a career-best 136 in 1993. The only year he didn't lead was 1991, yet that was the only year he was officially voted—not selected as a need player—to the Pro Bowl.

He left Buffalo and played one year in Atlanta, then another in Minnesota before retiring at the end of 1996.

He and his wife, Janine, and their two daughters, Alexandra and Gabrielle, moved to the Orlando area where Talley bought Sentry Barricade, a company that manufactures and leases barricades for road closures, detours and construction, among other things.

Talley has expressed an interest in coaching, but if he never makes it back into an NFL stadium, so be it. One stadium will always be home to Talley—Ralph Wilson Stadium in Buffalo where his name is affixed to the Bills' Wall of Fame.

"It means a lot to me," he said. "I don't think anyone can take as many memories away from that stadium as I did."

CHAPTER FIFTEEN

Steve Tasker

Position: Wide receiver/special teams
Number: 89
Years with Bills: 1986-97
Other teams: Oilers (1985-86)
College: Northwestern
Born: April 10, 1962
Birthplace: Smith Center, Kansas
Current residence: Orchard Park, New York
Current occupation: Football analyst—CBS

Steve is considered by many to be the greatest special teams player in NFL history…was credited with 204 tackles on kickoffs and punts, and he blocked seven punts in 195 career games…in 2000 he was voted by the Pro Football Hall of Fame voters to the All-Time NFL Team, where he joined only 26 other players…earned seven Pro Bowl invitations including six in a row from 1990-95…was the Pro Bowl MVP in 1993…finished his career with 51 receptions for 779 yards and nine TDs.

THIS IS STEVE TASKER

It's not like it hadn't happened before, so Steve Tasker simply shrugged off the indignant slight with the typically easy manner and choirboy smile that created the misunderstanding in the first place.

It was the middle of Super Bowl XXVIII week in Atlanta, and Tasker and his Buffalo teammates were heading to a meeting in one of the banquet rooms of the team's headquarter hotel, the Stouffer Waverly. Tasker was carrying his playbook in one hand, a Sony camcorder in the other, looking every bit like a star-struck fan as he videotaped the surroundings.

One of the security guards saw him coming and, thinking there was no way this five-foot-nine, 180-pound runt with the video camera could possibly be a player, muscled his way in front of Tasker, preventing him from entering the room.

When Tasker tried to convince him he was a member of the Bills, the guard replied, "Yeah, right. You fans will try anything. Get out of here." Just then, a few of the Bills, normal-sized NFL players with bulging necks and biceps, sidled up and informed the guard that yes indeed, this guy really was on the team. In fact, to that point, the guy you're laughing at has already played in four Pro Bowls and has re-defined the way people think about special teams.

"I can't blame them," Tasker said at the time. "I don't look like a football player. If I don't wear my uniform, nobody knows who I am. Even if I do wear my jersey, people say, 'Is Tasker your favorite player?' If I tell them I am Tasker, they say, 'You mean you're his little brother?' Fathers will come up with their sons, pat me on the back and say, 'See son, you don't have to be big or strong or fast to be in the NFL.' I don't know if I should thank them or what."

Tasker was never big or strong, but he was fast, tough, smart, and he had a heart the size of the Western hemisphere. Those attributes more than made up for his physical inadequacies and the fact that he looked like the boy next door.

The boy next door grew up as the boy next door in America's heartland in a small town called Leoti situated on the western edge of Kansas. There's not much to Leoti, the only incorporated town in 24-square mile Wichita County. It's a dot on the map where highways 96 and 25 intersect, and, as Tasker will say, "Except for the two highways, the roads beyond town turn into dirt." There's a few bars, a few auto parts stores, a few churches, a grocery store, a flashing light and a sign at that highway intersection that welcomes all visitors: "Leoti, Kansas: Home of STEVE TASKER, The 1993 Pro Bowl MVP."

Steve Tasker is considered by many football experts to be the finest special teams play-er in NFL history. **Courtesy of the Buffalo Bills**

Tasker's father was a Methodist minister, and while Leoti is where Tasker calls home, the Tasker clan—mom, dad, and four boys—moved around the state when he was growing up.

The Tasker boys were, to say the least, rambunctious. "You know the old joke about the worst kids in town being the preacher's kids," Tasker said. "Well, that was pretty much the case with us. When I lived in Kiowa, my three brothers and I set some kind of Kansas record for shattering rectory windows. We must have broken 25 windows out of the parsonage one year playing baseball, throwing stones and even with our heads."

Is it any wonder Tasker went on to become one of the greatest special teams players in history?

At Wichita County High School, he lettered in football and basketball, plus he ran track, and in 1980 he won four gold medals at the Kansas state track meet. When he wasn't starring on athletic fields, he was performing in lead roles for the high school productions of *Oliver* and *The Music Man*.

At only 140 pounds in his senior year, Broadway might have been a more likely destination for Tasker, but he was an athlete first, and when Southwestern College of Winfield and Dodge City Community College showed interest in him as a football player, he chose Dodge City and began plotting an unlikely course to the NFL.

He spent one season at Dodge City, then transferred to Northwestern where he majored in communications and played for coach Dennis Green, grabbing the attention of NFL scouts with his play on the kicking teams.

Houston picked him in the ninth round of the 1985 draft, No. 226 overall, and he played a little over a year before the Oilers made a huge mistake. They waived Tasker. Joe Faragalli, a Buffalo assistant coach who had worked for the Oilers the previous season and knew Tasker, saw his name come across the waiver wire and he walked into the office of his new boss, head coach Marv Levy, who had replaced the fired Hank Bullough a few days earlier.

Faragalli struggled to convince Levy how a five-foot-nine, 175-pound, ninth-round draft pick who had just been waived by a bad Houston team could help the Bills. Until, that is, he mentioned what a dynamo he would be on special teams.

"Why didn't you say that in the first place?" said Levy, who began his career as a special teams coach and learned under ex-Redskins coach George Allen the importance of the kicking game. Levy and Faragalli marched down to general manager Bill Polian's office and asked him to put in a claim for Tasker. Polian did, not knowing that Tasker would eventually play in seven Pro Bowls as the AFC's special teams representative.

"Most players hate going to special teams," said the man who put the special in special teams. "With me it was different. I found my niche and I was content with it."

Why not? It was quite a career for a guy from Leoti, Kansas.

GAME DAY SETTING

Tasker knew it was not an ordinary day when he arrived at Tampa Stadium and saw spectators and media walking through airport-like security devices and being patted down as if they were criminal suspects.

"We had a police escort to the stadium like we always do, but the game is 6:20 in the evening and at two o'clock we're headed over there and you can't get near the place," Tasker said. "The cops just jumped across the median and we're on the wrong side of the lane buzzing down the road. We didn't have to go through a metal detector like everybody else did, but that was just wild to see. I never gave security a thought until then."

Tasker knew it was not an ordinary day when he stepped out of the Buffalo locker room and made his typical walk down the tunnel and onto the field with Bills quarterback Jim Kelly, a ritual the two performed before every game.

"Kelly and I used to walk onto the field before everyone else because he was as superstitious as you could get," Tasker remembered. "Usually you walk out and the tunnel is empty, but that first Super Bowl it was packed. They have the felt ropes set up to make an aisle for us to get out and we start to go and I'm with Jim and it was literally like walking with a deity. There was like this 35-foot circle around him and everybody is focused on him and his presence kind of goes ahead of us as he's coming. It was unbelievable. We swing out onto the field and you could literally feel the attention of the world. I told Jim later I could have been blind and deaf and I still would have felt it. It was that electric, particularly walking with him. It was rock star stuff. It was pretty cool."

Tasker knew it was not an ordinary day when he was standing on the sideline during the national anthem, his eyes tantalized by the amazing sights and watered with overwhelming emotion.

"Whitney Houston sings the national anthem and it turns into a hit single, I mean she's phenomenal," said Tasker. "Then they have the flyover with the jets which you see a lot and it's usually no big deal, but then the attack helicopter flies over with a gun on it, with a soldier hanging out the side, low; low enough where you can tell the guy hadn't shaved that day and they flew it like they meant business.

"And then Whitney Houston hits the last note of the anthem and I look over at Larry Nemmers who's one of the officials and he's crying his eyes out. Marv is crying his eyes out. I turn around and look in the stands and everybody has a little American flag and they're waving it with one hand and wiping their eyes with the other."

The day of the Super Bowl for the participating teams is never an ordinary day, but what the Bills and New York Giants had to endure on that warm central Florida evening in January 1991 was a day like no other in NFL history.

Less than two weeks earlier, as the Bills and Giants were preparing for their respective conference championship games, President Bush the elder sent American troops into the Persian Gulf War and quite naturally, silly endeavors such as sporting events lost their importance—even the Super Bowl.

Despite worries that madman Saddam Hussein would authorize a terrorist attack in response to the bombs that were raining down on Baghdad, the NFL played on. Buffalo annihilated the Raiders, 51-3, and the Giants upset San Francisco, 15-13, to set up an all-New York State Super Bowl.

All week there was a noticeable pall cast over the Super Bowl festivities. People were toned down, respectful of the men and women risking their lives overseas, and there was a sense that the game might suffer as well. How could these two teams, despite the veteran leadership both possessed, function in this bubbling cauldron? Surely their performance would suffer.

But then the game began and those notions were quickly muted. The Bills and Giants attacked each other with a fury and the fans loved it. So many Super Bowls before and since had died under the weight of hype. This one thrived, and it became a game for the ages and the game of Tasker's life.

For three glorious hours, the Bills and Giants enabled America to divert its attention away from Desert Storm. For three glorious hours America did what America loved to do. It watched football, and what a football game it saw.

THE GAME

January 27, 1991
GIANTS 20, BILLS 19

Matt Bahr, the New York place kicker whose 21-yard field goal midway through the fourth quarter provided the Giants with the winning points in their heart-pounding 20-19 victory over the Bills in Super Bowl XXV, paid a visit to Buffalo's training camp in the summer of 2004.

Bahr, who lives in Pennsylvania, had done some off-season work with Bills' kicker Rian Lindell and when the Bills reported to training camp in early August at Rochester's St. John Fisher College, Lindell asked Bahr to come up and check on his mechanics.

One of the days Bahr was at camp, he ran into Tasker who, as the play-by-play announcer on the Bills' preseason telecasts, was familiarizing himself with the new Buffalo players. The two men couldn't resist talking about Super Bowl XXV.

"I said to Matt, 'Scott Norwood didn't lose that game for us, you won it,'" recalled Tasker. "And he said, 'What do you mean?' and I told him, 'You made two tackles on kickoff returns that if you didn't make them, it was a touchdown.'

He said, 'Yeah, I know I did. Nobody remembers that.'"

Given the way that game ended, can you blame anyone for that oversight?

Until recently, when New England's Adam Vinatieri began making a habit out of kicking last-play field goals to win Super Bowls, you could make a strong argument that the most dramatic Super Bowl of all was No. 25 between the Bills and Giants.

It came down to Norwood's 47-yard field goal attempt, still the only win-or-else field goal attempt in Super Bowl history. Remember, both of Vinatieri's winners, as well as the winner Baltimore's Jim O'Brien kicked in Super Bowl V, came with the score tied. Norwood's was win or lose. Make it and he's the all-time Buffalo hero. Miss it and he is what he is, fair or not, an all-time goat.

Of course, he missed, and while his teammates forgave him that very night and have never once pointed a finger at Norwood, that doesn't change the fact that that loss was the most painful in Bills history—for them and for their fans.

"I remember coming off the field, and it's the only time I ever lost a game in anything where I physically felt sick," Tasker said. "That didn't happen in Super Bowl XXVI, XXVII, or XXVIII. I never felt like that afterwards, even after we got beat 52-17 by the Cowboys [in XXVII]. But it did against the Giants because we were better than they were and we should have won."

One of the Bahr tackles Tasker referenced occurred on the opening kickoff when Don Smith found a seam but was tripped up by Bahr at the Bills' 34.

"It seemed like every time there was a kickoff or a punt in that game, on both sides, the last guy made the tackle," said Tasker. "I know Matt made two of those, and I remember making a tackle on Dave Meggett where if I didn't make the tackle, he was gone. I was getting my ass kicked on a double team and he was coming. They blocked me off and I dropped into a squat and dove between their legs to trip him up."

After the Giants took an early 3-0 lead on Bahr's 28-yard field goal, Jim Kelly connected with James Lofton on a 61-yard pass to position the Bills on the New York eight, but two Kelly incompletions forced Buffalo to settle for Norwood's tying 23-yard field goal.

The Bills then took command of the game in the second quarter as Kelly—at his no-huddling best—engineered a 12-play, 80-yard drive that included four passes to Andre Reed for 44 yards. Smith, a little-used running back, culminated the march with a one-yard touchdown plunge. Two possessions later Giants quarterback Jeff Hostetler stumbled to the ground in his own end zone and Bruce Smith fell on him for a safety to give the Bills a 12-3 lead.

With momentum clearly on their side, the Bills could have buried the Giants after the free kick, but their next two possessions resulted in punts, and after the second, Hostetler trotted onto the field with 3:49 left in the half. The Giants needed a spark, and the man who was filling in for injured starter Phil Simms provided it.

Hostetler, who had been unable to get much working to this point, suddenly found his groove. He completed five of eight passes during an 87-yard march, the last a 14-yard scoring toss to Stephen Baker with 25 seconds left in the half. Then New York received the second-half kickoff and embarked on a remarkable touchdown drive that consumed the first 9:29 of the third quarter. The 14-play, 75-yard journey was marked by a number of big plays, none bigger than Hostetler's 14-yard completion to Mark Ingram on a third-and-13 from the Buffalo 32 on which the Bills missed about five tackles. Eventually, Ottis Anderson crashed across the goal line from the 1 to give the Giants a 17-12 lead.

Bahr saved a touchdown when he tackled Al Edwards at the Bills' 40 on the ensuing kickoff, and while the Bills wound up punting on that series, they were back on the attack moments later when, late in the third quarter, Bruce Smith stuffed Anderson on a fourth-down play at the Bills 37.

Kelly—who had been on the field less than two minutes in the third quarter—rode that momentum swing to the go-ahead touchdown early in the fourth. He completed three quick passes for 32 yards, then watched as Thurman Thomas swept around right end for a 31-yard touchdown that put the Bills on top, 19-17.

Another long New York march, this one chewing up 7:32, resulted in Bahr kicking what turned out to be the winning 21-yard field goal with 7:20 left, and after an exchange of punts—Tasker making his big tackle to prevent Meggett from going the distance—the Bills wound up on their own 10-yard line with 2:16 left to play. Kelly entered the huddle and said, "This is what champions are made of. Let's be one."

Two Kelly scrambles and a 22-yard run on third down by Thomas put the ball at the 41 as a huge roar from the Buffalo contingent pierced the warm Tampa air. After another first down Kelly called his final timeout with 48 seconds remaining, and following a Keith McKeller reception, Thomas's last carry of a superb 190-yard total offense day netted 11 yards to the 29. However, when cornerback Mark Collins tackled him in bounds, the Bills were not going to be able to run another play. Kelly hustled to the line and spiked the ball to stop the clock with eight ticks left.

"I had positive thoughts," Norwood said of the kick. "I don't back away from kicks like this. It's something I've done my whole career. It's a kick I've made."

Just not on this night.

SINCE THE GAME

Tasker and the Bills would go on to play in three more Super Bowls, and they never came nearly as close to winning as they did that night in Tampa.

Steve Tasker joined the Bills in time for Marv Levy's first game in 1986, and both men retired after the 1997 season. **Courtesy of the Buffalo Bills**

"I realized at that point how long and how far we had come to get there, and all I could think about was now we've got to do it again," he said. "It took me a long time to get over that."

Tasker retired at the end of the 1997 season and made a smooth transition into the media world. Using his communications degree from Northwestern, Tasker worked for the ABC affiliate in Buffalo learning the ropes, then took his skills to the national level when he landed an analyst job on CBS broadcasts in 1998 and remains there today, working telecasts primarily with veteran Don Criqui.

He, his wife Sarah, and their five children make their home in the Buffalo suburb of East Aurora, mainly because it reminds Tasker of Leoti.

"Buffalo's a great city," he said. "In fact, my wife and I, when we first got there, we said it reminded us a lot of Leoti because when you live in Buffalo, like you do in Leoti, it's because you grew up there. Your dad went to high school there. You grew up there. You stayed in Leoti. That's the way it is in Buffalo."

CHAPTER SIXTEEN

Jim Kelly

Position: Quarterback
Number: 12
Years with Bills: 1986-96
Other teams: None
College: Miami, Florida
Born: February 14, 1960
Hometown: East Brady, Pennsylvania
Current residence: Orchard Park, New York
Current occupation: Retired player

Jim became the fourth member of the Bills organization to be enshrined in the Pro Football Hall of Fame in 2002, one year after having his name added to the Bills Wall of Fame at Ralph Wilson Stadium…earned five Pro Bowl invitations and was the game's MVP in 1990…record as a starting quarterback was 101-59 in the regular season, 9-8 in the postseason…is the Bills' all-time leader in pass attempts (4,780), completions (2,874), yards (35,467) and touchdowns (237)…began pro career in the USFL and threw for 9,842 yards in just two seasons with the Houston Gamblers.

THIS IS JIM KELLY

Jim Kelly and toughness go together about as well as peanut butter and jelly, his sandwich of choice as a youngster growing up in tiny East Brady, Pennsylvania.

The majestic spirals that he threw, so powerful that they seemed to cut through the bitingly cold Orchard Park air with a smile, will never be forgotten. Nor will the sight of Kelly, after every touchdown pass that he tossed at Rich Stadium, pointing up to his luxury box where his family sat every Sunday and giving them a heartfelt salute.

The accomplishments blow you away—six AFC East division titles, four AFC championships, five invitations to the Pro Bowl, and now, a bronzed bust in the Pro Football Hall of Fame. The numbers are equally impressive—2,874 completions, 4,780 attempts, 35,647 yards, 237 touchdowns and an 84.4 passer rating which are all Bills records.

There was the swagger—the brashness. The absolute confidence that was mistaken as arrogance when he first blew into Buffalo in the summer of 1986 charged with rejuvenating not only a sad-sack football franchise, but a sagging city.

But more than anything, it was Kelly's toughness that set him apart from almost every quarterback who ever played the game.

His Bills coach, Marv Levy, has said he was "the toughest player I ever coached." His teammates, many of them very tough in their own rite, readily concur. "He was a linebacker in a quarterback's position," said the ultimate warrior, Darryl Talley, a man who never missed a game during his 12 years in Buffalo. "I call him Heathcliff. He's a cat who thinks he's a dog."

Oh, Kelly was tough, there's no denying it. However, he has nothing on his son, Hunter, a little boy who has raised the toughness meter to astronomical standards, and Kelly made sure everyone knew that on the afternoon that he was inducted into the Hall of Fame.

"It has been written throughout my career that toughness is my trademark," Kelly said. "Well, the toughest person I've ever met in my life is my hero, my soldier, my son, Hunter."

Hunter James Kelly was born on Valentine's Day 1997, his father's 37th birthday, a seemingly healthy seven pound, 14-ounce boy. He was supposed to have died somewhere around Valentine's Day 1998.

Less than six months into his life Hunter was diagnosed with infantile Krabbe Disease, an insidious and rare degenerative disorder of the nervous system that typically kills its victims in the first 13 months.

You want to talk about tough? This little boy has lived trapped inside a body that cannot function, with a mind that cannot develop. He has endured an unfathomable existence, yet he fights on. The miracle that is his life continues today as he turned eight on February 14, 2005, the oldest living person diagnosed with the disease that afflicts only one out of every 100,000 to 200,000 live births.

Hunter has never spoken. He has never smiled. He has never walked. He will never do any of those things as long as he lives—but he lives, and he inspires. He means more to his father than anything Jim Kelly—the toughest football player of his generation and many others—ever accomplished on the gridiron.

Hunter's condition prevents him from dreaming a child's dreams. Dreaming is all his father ever did as a little boy, and just about every one of Jim's dreams—except the one about playing catch with his son—has come true.

Jim was one of six sons born to Joe and Alice Kelly of East Brady, Pennsylvania, a picturesque but mostly desolate town along the Allegheny River about 65 miles northeast of Pittsburgh. There are no traffic lights in East Brady, just stop signs. The coal mines are vacant, the rubber plant that once was the town's lifeblood is closed. As Kelly wrote in his autobiography, *Armed and Dangerous*, "Basically what you do in East Brady—although I'm proud to call it my hometown—is to try to make a better life for yourself."

And that's what he did.

Kelly became the star quarterback for East Brady High School, passing for 3,915 yards and 44 TDs in his career. He also starred on the basketball team averaging 23 points and 20 rebounds as a senior. But football was his destiny, and not as a linebacker as Penn State's Joe Paterno envisioned.

Kelly had longed to play at nearby Penn State, but Paterno was convinced the rugged kid was better suited to linebacker. Kelly disagreed, accepted a scholarship to the University of Miami, and he became the first—and most prominent—in a steady line of Hurricane quarterbacks to make it to the NFL.

He helped turn the Miami program around, and one year after he graduated, the Hurricanes won the national championship. By then Kelly had been drafted in the first round by the Bills, spurned Buffalo to play for Houston of the USFL, and was about to set the football world aflame with the run-and-shoot Gamblers.

In two seasons at the Astrodome, he passed for nearly 10,000 yards and 83 touchdowns and became the scourge of Buffalo because without him, the quarterback-poor Bills suffered through back-to-back 2-14 seasons. However, the USFL folded its operation in the summer of 1986 and Kelly's NFL rights were still owned by Buffalo. General manager Bill Polian knew signing Kelly was the first step toward rebuilding the team, and when the Bills ponied up a five-year, $8 million contract, Kelly finally agreed to come to Western New York and all was forgiven.

He was looked upon as the savior, and though one fan went a bit far with signage that read "Kelly is God," Kelly nonetheless delivered salvation to a victory-starved populace. Over the next 11 years, Kelly—with help

When Jim Kelly came to Buffalo in 1986, the Bills were an NFL laughingstock.
When he retired, he'd led them to six AFC-East titles and four AFC championships.
Courtesy of the Buffalo Bills

from a remarkably talented team constructed by the front office triumvirate
of Levy, Polian, and John Butler—lorded over the golden era of Bills football.

"It's funny how things turn out sometimes," Kelly said. "I'm so happy Ralph Wilson didn't listen to me and trade me. I was doing my best to make sure it wouldn't work out between me and the Bills. I wanted them to trade me to a team like the Raiders or the Steelers. I wanted to go someplace where I would have a chance to win, and to be honest, I didn't think the Bills were committed to winning."

GAME DAY SETTING

The Bills, as Kelly later found out, were committed to winning. It just didn't happen right away.

In Kelly's first season the team struggled to a 4-12 record, but Kelly was a beacon of hope as he set a team record with 285 pass completions, and his 3,593 passing yards were the second most in team history.

In the strike-marred 1987 season, Buffalo improved to 7-8 with a roster that had been greatly upgraded, and then the Bills captured the AFC East division title in 1988, the first of six they would win under Kelly's stewardship, before losing the AFC Championship Game at Cincinnati.

After taking a step back during the soap operatic 1989 season when the Bills won another AFC East title despite incessant internal bickering, only to lose in the divisional round of the playoffs to Cleveland, Kelly came to a pivotal crossroad.

By now Kelly had become the biggest star on the Buffalo sports scene since O.J. Simpson in the mid-1970s, and his status grew exponentially in 1990 when he guided the Bills to their first appearance in the Super Bowl. But before that ticket to Tampa was punched, Kelly learned a valuable lesson. He was the epicenter of the team's success, but he was not the sole reason for it, and once this realization struck him and he corralled his energetic ego, the Bills soared to previously unimagined heights.

"It's hard to describe," he said of the role he played in rescuing the Bills from the abyss. "I always knew, and I was always brought up believing, that you can't do things alone. I know I was a key ingredient because of the position I played, and I knew that in order for the Bills to go anywhere they had to have a top quarterback. But I also take great pride in knowing that I was one of our leaders on the team. I was able to get people to not so much follow me, but join me, and I had enough people to join me."

The Bills advanced to the Super Bowl following the 1990 season and that heartbreaking loss provided enormous motivation for the team heading into 1991, a year in which Kelly engineered the greatest offensive display in Buffalo history.

This was the year Buffalo went exclusively to the no-huddle offense with Kelly calling his own plays and swashbuckling up and down NFL fields as exhausted defenses tried to keep pace. The Bills set still-unbroken team records for points (458), touchdowns (58), first downs (359) and total yards

(6,252), and Kelly set career highs for yards passing (3,884), completion percentage (64.1), attempts (474), completions (304) and touchdowns (33).

"We were so successful, and we really had the ballplayers to do anything we wanted," said offensive coordinator Ted Marchibroda. "It was a lot of fun. It was the best offense I've ever been associated with, it really was."

In the season opener the Bills exploded for a 35-31 victory over Miami as they totaled 33 first downs and 582 yards, single-game team records that still stand. The Bills' offense was the talk of the league, and up next were the Pittsburgh Steelers, the Steelers Kelly once rooted for as a kid.

THE GAME

September 8, 1991
BILLS 52, STEELERS 34

Kelly used to sit in grammar school classes and practice signing his autograph. Even then he knew someday kids just like him would be asking for his signature. It was his dream to play quarterback in the NFL, just like his idol, Steelers quarterback Terry Bradshaw.

The Steelers were his team. They were just about everyone's team in East Brady. Bradshaw, Lynn Swann, John Stallworth, Franco Harris, and Rocky Bleier on offense, Mean Joe Greene, Jack Lambert, Mel Blount, Jack Ham and the rest of the Steel Curtain defense.

The Steelers won four Super Bowls in a six-year period in the 1970s, the NFL's team of the decade during the decade of Kelly's adolescence. Pittsburgh was the only place Kelly ever wanted to play. That is, until he signed with the Bills. Then the Steelers became the team he couldn't wait to beat.

"When I was a kid I grew up watching the Steelers with the terrible towel and Myron Cope on the radio and watching my idol Terry Bradshaw," said Kelly. "Every time the Steelers were playing I was watching the game and I wanted to play for the Steelers. That was my dream as a kid. In Western New York, you dream about playing for the Bills, in Wisconsin it's the Packers, and for me it was the Steelers.

"So that day we're playing the Steelers in Orchard Park, my whole family was there, my friends from my hometown were there, and it turned out to be the best game of my career."

The game of his life. The final was 52-34 as he threw for 363 yards and six touchdowns, four of the scoring passes going to Don Beebe.

"When you throw six, I guess you should remember them, but I had problems remembering a lot of things," Kelly said with a laugh. "And not only is my memory going, I have to use reading glasses now, too. I don't remember most of them, but I know it was a special day. I flew my brothers in for almost every game and my mom and dad were there. But for me, when you beat the Pittsburgh Steelers, that was a game I'll never forget."

These were not the Steel Curtain Steelers of the 1970s, but they were a formidable group. The year before Chuck Noll's defense led the NFL in fewest yards and passing yards allowed and was No. 3 in points allowed. In 16 games, Pittsburgh yielded only nine touchdown passes.

Kelly had a third of that by halftime, two-thirds of that by the end of the day as the Bills put up the second highest point total in team history and surpassed 500 yards of total offense and 30 first downs for the second week in a row.

"There was a lot of ad-libbing in that game, especially with Don Beebe," he remembered. "We watched film and we knew if we sent Beebe on quick posts that we'd be able to beat Rod Woodson. It didn't make Andre Reed that happy because I was calling these plays and giving Don individual routes and they turned out to be the right ones."

The onslaught began midway through the first quarter when Kelly fired a 53-yard TD pass to James Lofton who beat Woodson. After Scott Norwood kicked a 50-yard field goal and Pittsburgh's Gary Anderson answered with a 25-yarder, Kelly and Beebe connected for the first two times on passes of 34 and 14 yards, both on last-second route alterations. Beebe was supposed to run outs on both plays, but when Kelly got to the line, he audibled and sent Beebe over the middle on posts, and the result was 14 points and a 24-3 lead.

"They left me one-on-one a lot, and Jim saw me open and got me the ball," Beebe said after the game. "Jim is the best quarterback in the league as far as seeing the whole field."

That's what made the no-huddle so lethal. Kelly was in control on the field and had the freedom to make adjustments like that. In an era when coaches controlled every aspect of the game, Kelly was a throwback to a time in football when the quarterback was the general who called the plays.

"Jim liked to run it much faster than any quarterback I ever had," said offensive coordinator Ted Marchibroda. "He would change the play; the only difference is that he'd change it quicker than what you're seeing today. People might think he called one play and ran it, but that wasn't the case at all."

Kelly's fourth touchdown pass was a 15-yarder to Reed that extended the lead to 31-10 early in the third quarter, but the Steelers responded with 17 straight points before the period ended, including linebacker Bryan Hinkle's 57-yard return for a touchdown of a poorly thrown Kelly interception.

However, the Bills erupted for 21 points in less than six minutes to put the game away. Kelly and Beebe hooked up twice again on scoring passes of 11 and four yards, and cornerback Nate Odomes returned a Bubby Brister interception 32 yards for a touchdown that made it 52-27.

The Steelers were shell-shocked when the final gun sounded. "They made us look like little kids out there," said Woodson. "They came out with that no-huddle, or whatever they call it, and it really winds the defense. I was tired."

So was Kelly after completing a career-best 31 passes out of 43 attempts.

"When the game was over I had six touchdown passes and I couldn't believe it," said Kelly. "I did it in front of a lot of my hometown people who traveled up to Buffalo. When I went home after that season, that's all everyone wanted to talk about was us playing against the Steelers and whipping them that day."

SINCE THE GAME

Kelly selected Marv Levy to be his presenter at his Hall of Fame induction, and as he always did, Levy rose to the occasion with a heartfelt speech that encapsulated the very essence of Kelly.

"Never mind his eye-popping statistics, he never cared about them anyway," Levy said. "Jim cared about winning, and he was a winner. He cared about his team and about his teammates. He cared about his wonderful family, and about our loyal and enthusiastic Buffalo Bills fans. He cared about his community, and he showed it.

"Never mind about his arm, it was great, but what was really noteworthy about Jim was his heart. Jim Kelly's heart was as stout as a nose tackle's butt. His qualities, he had them all. Toughness. Leadership. Was he good in the locker room? Heck no, his locker was a mess! Our equipment managers, Hojo and Woody, were good in the locker room; Jim led by his actions out on the playing field."

And it is those same qualities that guide Kelly in the most important quest of his life. The touchdown passes have faded from his memory, as have the triumphs and defeats, even the Super Bowl losses. Today, Kelly is doing work far more meaningful than taking the Bills on a game-winning touchdown drive in the final minutes.

At the time Hunter was diagnosed, the Kellys were told there was nothing they could do for their child. He was going to die because there were no known treatments, and all they could do was make him as comfortable as possible as his life withered away.

That was an unacceptable course of action for a man so competitive, so used to trying his best no matter how dire the circumstances. Jim and his wife, Jill, had to do something, so they established the Hunter's Hope Foundation.

"I was mad at the world," Kelly said, "and tired of people telling me, 'Your son is here for a reason.' Now I understand it, why he is here; it's to help other kids."

Kelly and Don Beebe celebrate one of the four touchdowns they connected for in a 52-34 victory over Pittsburgh. **Courtesy of the Buffalo Bills**

THIS IS MARV LEVY

Sam and Ida Levy were so proud of their only son, Marv.
A star athlete at South Shore High School in Chicago; World War II veteran, though he never actually fought overseas; star member of the Coe College football and track teams where he also served one year as student council president; magna cum laude graduate, which earned him a Phi Beta Kappa key and admission to Harvard Law School.

Harvard Law. Their son Marv.

"In the middle of my third week at Harvard Law School I made the decision that I wanted to be a football coach," Levy said. "Although my body was in the classrooms, my heart kept drifting to the playing fields."

How do you tell your parents that you would rather coach football than pursue the practice of law? A football coach?

If you are Marv Levy, and your parents are Sam and Ida Levy, you just tell them. And then you listen to your father, the wisest man you've ever known, say to you, "If that's what you've decided you are going to do, just make damn sure you do a good job of it. And I know you will."

Marv Levy never knew an occasion when his father—an English immigrant who had put on hold his own high school athletic career to heroically fight for his adopted country in World War I—was wrong. And Sam wasn't this time, either.

At South Shore High Marv played basketball and football, and after a slow start academically, he became an honor student. College would have to wait, though, because he joined the Army Air Corps upon graduation in 1943. While 20/40 vision grounded his dream of flying war planes and prevented him from following in his father's gallant boots, Levy served his country as a weather watcher at various stations in Florida until his discharge in 1946.

Levy set off for the University of Wyoming, but after a semester he realized the demands of the football program infringed too heavily on his studying, so he transferred to Coe College in Cedar Rapids, Iowa.

At Coe he played football, ran the quarter-mile in track, and during his senior year when several players were dropped from the basketball team due to training violations, he was recruited from the intramural league and earned a letter.

It was also at Coe where, despite his obvious love of academics and his desire to attend Harvard Law School, he developed his affinity for the coaching profession. His football coach, Dick Clausen, and his track coach, Harris Lamb, were monumental men of character in Levy's eyes, and being around them made him think coaching could be a wonderful way to make a living in this world.

Marv Levy coached 47 years in high school, college, the CFL, the USFL, and the NFL—but his greatest success came during his 11-plus year tenure with Buffalo.
Courtesy of the Buffalo Bills

And so came that autumn day at Cambridge, Massachusetts in 1950 when he realized his future would not be spent in courtrooms but on ball fields. Levy asked for (and was granted) a transfer to Harvard's Graduate School of Arts and Sciences. With the intention of teaching and coaching by the following fall, he set out on a frenetic pursuit of his master's degree in one year's time. Somehow he managed to survive a grueling class load, earning straight A's, and was able to complete his master's thesis that brought with it a coveted Harvard diploma that remained affixed to his mother's bedroom wall all of her remaining years.

His coaching odyssey began in 1951 at St. Louis Country Day, a prep school in St. Louis, and then he moved up to college football when Clausen summoned him back to Coe to serve as one of his assistants. He would later become head coach at New Mexico, California and William and Mary before breaking into the NFL as an assistant coach for the Philadelphia Eagles in 1969 and later under George Allen with the Los Angeles Rams and Washington Redskins.

He needed to move north of the border in order to attain his first head coaching job in the pros and his five-year term with Montreal of the Canadian league yielded two Grey Cup championships and ultimately paved his way back to the NFL when he was hired as head coach of the Kansas City Chiefs in 1978.

Levy's Chiefs improved each of his first four years, but the NFL players' strike of 1982 ruined his team and he was fired at the end of the year by owner Lamar Hunt who years later admitted he made a grave mistake letting Levy go.

After working in the USFL and later in broadcasting, Levy made his return to the NFL sidelines at the age of 61 when Buffalo owner Ralph Wilson hired him midway through 1986 to turn around his bumbling Bills. So began the golden era of Bills football, and it began with a coaching tenet Levy had gleaned from Clausen: "What it takes to win is simple, but it isn't easy."

Eleven magnificent years later, Levy retired as one of the finest coaches the NFL has ever known, one of only 20 who have been enshrined in the Hall of Fame through 2005. On that day in Canton, Ohio, Bill Polian—whom Levy had chosen as his presenter—summed up best what Levy meant to the Bills and to football.

"It is said that leadership is that unique quality which enables special people to stand up and pull the rest of us over the horizon," Polian said. "By that or any other definition, Marv Levy is one of the greatest leaders this game has ever known."

GAME DAY SETTING

On a mid-December day in 1943, Levy was riding on a train from Chicago with a group of other recent military enlistees bound for Greensboro, North Carolina where they would begin basic training for the Army Air Corps. The 18-year-old cadet-in-waiting opened a book containing English poetry given to him by his mother when she dropped him off at Union Station that morning, and he was captivated by one particular piece of prose written in tribute to a 16th-century Scottish warrior named Sir Andrew.

"Fight on, my men,
A little I'm hurt, but not yet slain,

I'll just lie down, and bleed awhile,
And then I'll rise and fight again."

Forty-seven years and one month later, Levy was laying in his Tampa, Florida hotel room bed, unable to find sleep after the most gut-wrenching defeat of his four-decade coaching career, Buffalo's 20-19 loss to the New York Giants in Super Bowl XXV.

After hours of tossing and turning, the game's dramatic events reverberating inside his head, Levy's thought process suddenly veered in a different direction, and that poem, for some reason, popped into his head.

It immediately struck him that he must share those words with his equally despondent players, because those words so accurately described the hurt the Bills were feeling, but at the same time pointed to a future that could be filled with promise if they could find it in their hearts and minds to "rise and fight again."

For the remainder of his tenure in Buffalo, that poem wound up on the locker room bulletin board after every one of the Bills' disheartening defeats, its purpose to remind the players that they might bleed for a little while, but there were other battles to fight.

Levy's sharing of that poem set the tone for the 1991 season. Many teams might have crumbled after such a bitter loss as they had suffered in Tampa. The Bills grew stronger.

"The people not close to the team don't understand what it took for Marv to get everyone on the team to get over the hurt," special teams star Mark Pike said. "His example and his message helped us come back with the same drive and determination over and over. He was awesome at that."

With the no-huddle offense operating at peak efficiency, the Bills rolled to five straight victories to begin the season, and following an embarrassing 33-6 loss in Kansas City on *Monday Night Football,* the Bills reeled off another five-game winning streak to improve to 10-1.

They wound up 13-3, AFC East division champs again, and after a bye week, the Bills played host to the Chiefs with the stakes just a bit higher than they had been back on that Monday night in October. Just as the game at Arrowhead three months earlier, this one was no contest, only this time it was Buffalo laughing at the end of the day. The final was 37-14, and it wasn't even that close, and the Bills had just one more hurdle to clear on their mission of reaching Minneapolis for Super Bowl XXVI: John Elway and the Denver Broncos.

"It was a long, hard road we had to travel to get to that point," said Levy. "We had been immersed ever since the end of the previous season, and we had licked our wounds. By the time we were playing that championship game, those thoughts were subdued. It wasn't a matter of gliding back to the Super Bowl. Every game we had worked and prepared hard for."

THE GAME

January 12, 1992
BILLS 10, BRONCOS 7

Levy, the only coach among the 20 Bills luminaries highlighted in this book, was asked what he thought the game of his life was. It wasn't hard to come up with No. 1.

"The Houston comeback game, of course," Levy said.

Sorry Marv, Frank Reich already claimed that one.

"Well, certainly the first Super Bowl against the Giants," he offered.

Steve Tasker jumped on that one.

"OK, how about the 51-3 AFC Championship Game against the Raiders," he said.

Um, Darryl Talley.

Obviously there was bound to be some overlap in this project, and Levy—who had just finished writing his autobiography *Where Else Would You Rather Be?* (Sports Publishing)—understood the process. So, making like his quarterback, Jim Kelly, he called a nifty audible.

"You know what," Levy said. "One game that probably isn't being talked about is our second AFC Championship Game when we beat Denver, 10-7."

He was right. No claims staked on that one, and so, by default, Levy chose the game that catapulted the Bills into their second consecutive Super Bowl, a nail-biting, surprisingly low-scoring tussle at Rich Stadium, as the game of his life.

Despite its lack of offense, Levy said: "In my 47 years of coaching this game has to rank as one of the five most exciting in my career. Every snap was drama."

Correct again. For a 10-7 game, the Buffalo-Denver showdown for AFC supremacy was filled with histrionics.

"It was Kelly vs. Elway, what a shootout, right," Levy said. "It was a scoreless game late into the third quarter."

Who would have believed it? A defensive struggle in Rich Stadium—otherwise known as the Palace of Points.

The Bills of Jim Kelly, Thurman Thomas, Andre Reed, James Lofton, and one of the best offensive lines in football, against the Broncos of John Elway, Vance Johnson, Shannon Sharpe, Gaston Green, Steve Sewell and an equally proficient offensive line.

Bring your calculators? How about an abacus instead.

"Surprise, surprise, surprise," said linebacker Darryl Talley of the way the game turned into a defensive struggle.

How about some more nuttiness?

• David Treadwell, Denver's normally reliable placekicker who had been the hero a week earlier in the Broncos' victory over Houston, missed three field goals in the first half, two bouncing off the right upright.

• The Bills' linebacker who made perhaps the biggest defensive play of the 1991 season was not Cornelius Bennett, Shane Conlan or Talley, but Carlton Bailey, who intercepted a tipped Elway pass and ran 11 yards for the Bills' lone touchdown.

• Scott Norwood, clearly over his Super Bowl miss from a year earlier, kicked a 45-yard field goal from the right hash mark, on a windy day, in a pressure-packed situation, to provide the eventual winning points with 4:18 left to play.

• And the Bills' defensive back who killed Denver's final chance at victory with 1:28 remaining by forcing and then recovering a fumble wasn't Nate Odomes, Leonard Smith or Mark Kelso, but Kirby Jackson.

"It wasn't the stars who won it that day," said Levy. "We had a lot of stars on our team, but on that day it was the relative unknowns who provided the heroics."

A Buffalo offense that had scored a still-standing franchise record 458 points was handcuffed by a Denver defense that ranked No. 1 in the AFC, No. 5 overall. At halftime, the Bills had three first downs and 58 total yards.

By the end of the day Kelly had completed just 13 of 25 passes for 117 yards and was intercepted twice, and Thomas was held to 72 yards rushing on 26 attempts, breaking his playoff streak of four consecutive 100-yard games. The Bills gained a mere 213 yards, made just 12 first downs, and failed to score an offensive touchdown at Rich Stadium for the first time in more than three years.

Yet they won the game because the Buffalo defense—an unfair victim of the Bills' quick-strike offense because it had to play so many minutes and downs and often allowed gobs of yards and points—came through with its finest effort of the year. Elway passed for just 121 yards before exiting with a deep thigh bruise early in the fourth quarter, and the Broncos rushed for only 81 yards and had two hugely costly turnovers.

"No one ever thought it would be a close game and no one ever thought that we wouldn't score a touchdown, but things happen," defensive end Bruce Smith said. "We were able to come up with enough big plays."

Begin with Bailey.

The unheralded fourth-year linebacker intercepted an Elway pass that was tipped by Jeff Wright and rumbled into the end zone to give the Bills a 7-0 lead with 5:28 remaining in the third quarter. It was second-and-10 at the Denver 19 and Elway dropped back and tried to set up a screen in the middle of the field. Wright broke through the line and pressured Elway, then instinctively stopped his rush and played pass defense. The unsuspecting Elway threw the ball right at him, Wright deflected it into the air, and Bailey caught it on the fly and went in for the score.

"I didn't recognize the tip right away," Bailey said. "I heard it and I looked up and saw the ball." And the next thing he saw was the red paint in the end zone and a tidal wave of glee rolling down from the sold-out crowd of more than 80,000.

The Bills fed off that play, thwarting a pair of Denver possessions, and the offense finally put together a scoring drive that resulted in Norwood's clutch field goal that produced a seemingly safe 10-0 lead.

By then Elway was out of the game and soon-to-be-retired back-up Gary Kubiak was in for the Broncos. Looking like a man who wasn't ready to call it quits, Kubiak drove Denver 85 yards in eight plays against Buffalo's prevent defense, capping the march with a three-yard touchdown run on a designed quarterback draw with 1:43 remaining.

"All we had to do to wrap up the game was recover the onside kick everyone knew they were going to attempt," said Levy. "They kicked, we all scrambled, and they recovered it."

However, on the first play from scrimmage Kubiak swung a pass into the flat to Steve Sewell and as the lumbering back was heading up field after the catch Jackson slammed into him and jarred the ball loose, then fell on the fumble to preserve the victory. When Jackson got up he was almost knocked back down by the gale force sigh of relief that blew through the stadium.

> *"Fight on, my men,*
> *A little I'm hurt, but not yet slain,*
> *I'll just lie down, and bleed awhile,*
> *And then I'll rise and fight again."*

They had fought, they were hurt, and they had bled following the haunting loss to the Giants in Super Bowl XXV. Yet they rose and fought again, which is what those Bills' teams of Levy always did.

"We were going back to the Super Bowl," Levy said.

SINCE THE GAME

Everyone knows what happened. Another loss. This time 37-24 to the Washington Redskins.

"It had been a noble effort on the part of our players," Levy said. "After losing a Super Bowl they had rededicated themselves to doing all that it takes to get back there again."

The Bills would go back twice more. And lose twice more.

Levy remained as Buffalo's coach through 1997. When he decided to retire at the age of 72, his resume included eight playoff teams in 11 seasons, six AFC East titles, four AFC championships, one NFL and three AFC coach of the year awards, and a Bills-record 123 coaching victories.

He still misses coaching nearly eight years after his farewell. Though he turned 80 in August 2005, he remains active in the media as a football ana-

Marv Levy won 154 games as an NFL coach (123 with the Bills)—his accomplishments were recognized when he was inducted into the Pro Football Hall of Fame in 2001. **Courtesy of Robert L. Smith (Orchard Park, NY)**

lyst and broadcaster including an association with the Bills as the color man on their preseason telecasts.

Another of the favorite sayings of Dick Clausen, Levy's old college coach at Coe, was, "What you do should speak so loudly that no one can hear what you say."

Levy's actions and his accomplishments screamed louder than a rock concert. However, anyone who has ever been associated with this sage never passed up an opportunity to listen to what he was saying.

CHAPTER EIGHTEEN

Frank Reich

Position: Quarterback
Number: 14
Years with Bills: 1985-94
Other teams: Panthers (1995), Jets (1996), Lions (1997-98)
College: Maryland
Born: December 4, 1961
Birthplace: Freeport, New York
Current residence: Charlotte, North Carolina
Current occupation: Director—Reformed Theological Seminary, Charlotte

Before directing Buffalo to the greatest comeback in NFL history in the 1992 playoffs against Houston, Frank guided Maryland to the greatest comeback victory in college football history in 1984 as the Terps came from 31-0 down to beat Miami…during his career he completed 508 of 932 passes (54.5 percent) for 6,075 yards with 40 touchdowns and 36 interceptions.

THIS IS FRANK REICH

As Frank Reich was throwing touchdown pass after touchdown pass, the Buffalo Bills were in the midst of pulling off the most implausible victory the NFL has ever known. He didn't have time to consider the ramifications of what was taking place.

In a purely football sense, a miracle was occurring at Rich Stadium on that January 1993 afternoon when the Bills, after falling behind Houston, 35-3, rallied to defeat the Oilers in overtime, 41-38. No team had ever come from further behind to win, and unless in the unlikely event the feat is ever topped, it will be known as the greatest comeback in NFL history.

In the hours and days that followed Steve Christie's game-winning field goal, as the euphoria of the victory faded, it began to resonate in Reich's mind and heart and soul just how meaningful this football game would become.

Never mind the score and the depths from which the Bills climbed; never mind the heroes, of which Reich was certainly one; never mind the prominent shelf space the game tape now occupies in the vault at NFL Films. This was more than just one of the greatest football games ever played.

Reich knew that what happened on that green rectangular swatch of gridiron would become a valuable tool in terms of the life lessons it would teach, and that perhaps those in need of hope and determination and strength and courage would now have a reference point.

"I just found out my mom has cancer," Reich revealed in the summer of 2004. "We were talking and she made reference to the comeback game because a friend of hers had said, 'Your son came back from that and you can come back from this.' She was using that game, my experience, in a positive sense. I thought about that, and I've learned so much from my mom, and here was a chance where I could offer her some advice and I said, 'Mom, that's a good metaphor, a good illustration, but let me remind you what the key to that was. It was one play at a time.'

"There's no guarantees on winning or losing the game of life or whether she'll beat cancer and be a cancer survivor, but the approach is to persevere one day a time, one victory at a time. If she can just achieve little victories along the way, that's the culmination of a mindset that can bring about a great comeback."

Reich was born in Freeport, New York, but his mother and father, Pat and Frank Sr., packed up their newborn son and moved to Lebanon, Pennsylvania because the small town near Harrisburg was a more desirable place to raise a family.

Pat was a health and physical education teacher at the middle school Frank and her other two children, Joe and Cyndee, attended. Frank Sr., cap-

Frank Reich authored the greatest comeback victory in college football history nine years before repeating that feat in the NFL. **Courtesy of the Buffalo Bills**

tain of the 1955 Penn State football team, went on to become a high school teacher and football coach and later an assistant coach at Lebanon Valley College.

The Reich children adhered to strict values that revolved around their belief in God and the importance of family, and regardless of what they were going to do in their lives, God and family would always come first and second.

"I don't know why certain things happen, and I don't think I can expect to know why everything happens," said Reich. "We just can't comprehend why He does what He does. But I know He was very much a part of that comeback game, and more importantly He's very much a part of my life. My priorities are God, and then family, and then everything else. That's been drilled into my mind since I was a child."

Reich played football at Cedar Crest High School, then attended the University of Maryland where he spent most of his college career backing up his roommate, Boomer Esiason. Except, that is, for the day in his senior season of 1984 when he provided a glimpse into the future by engineering the greatest comeback victory in college football history.

His devout Christian faith took on new meaning when he came off the bench at the start of the third quarter with his Terrapins trailing the defending national champion Miami Hurricanes, 31-0, at the Orange Bowl, and rallied them to an unfathomable 42-40 victory.

Before the Miami game, that career seemed unlikely to be one of a professional football player, but Reich opened some eyes with what you would have thought was a once-in-a-lifetime performance, and the Bills ultimately selected him in the third round of the 1985 draft.

Like most rookie quarterbacks, he languished on the bench his first year, then was hoping to take a step forward in 1986 and compete for the starting job, which he was doing in training camp at Fredonia State College. However, Buffalo's first-round choice in 1983, a guy named Jim Kelly who had spurned Buffalo and gone to play in the USFL for a couple years, joined the Bills just three weeks before the start of the 1986 season when the USFL folded.

Kelly instantly became the Bills quarterback, and while he would go on to forge a Pro Football Hall of Fame career, Reich spent the next eight years as Kelly's caddy, and he earned a reputation as one of the finest relievers the NFL has known.

"Frank is a person of high character," said former Bills coach Marv Levy. "He's a well-rounded family man who's deeply religious. Sometimes the guy who has other things in his life doesn't clutch up. It makes him be able to retain an equilibrium."

GAME DAY SETTING

The bedlam in the locker room had subsided, the tears of joy and disbelief had dried up, the grudging congratulatory postgame handshake from University of Miami coach Jimmy Johnson had transpired, and now the 22-year-old Reich was left with the daunting task of trying to make sense out of what he and his Maryland teammates had just accomplished.

"It's something you wish everybody could experience so they could have the privilege, the feeling of how it rushes in you," said Reich, trying to express the burst of adrenaline that coursed through his veins as he was leading the Terrapins to their comeback victory over the Hurricanes. "We did the impossible, because no one in the world would think we could come back from that many points behind against Miami," Reich continued.

The rally earned a place in college football lore as the greatest comeback ever, and it made an unlikely hero out of a young man who just weeks earlier was beginning to think about what he was going to do with the rest of his life. And football wasn't in the mix.

Reich had waited patiently for his chance to shine at Maryland, and once Boomer Esiason graduated to the NFL in 1983, Reich was going to be the starting quarterback in 1984. However, a shoulder injury knocked him out of commission and when his replacement, another future Buffalo Bill, Stan Gelbaugh, enjoyed some success, coach Bobby Ross decided to stick with him even when Reich was healthy enough to play.

Linda Fick, Reich's girlfriend from their Lebanon days at Cedar Crest when he was a football star and she a cheerleader, had recently told him: "It's always darkest before the dawn." During the time he sat out because of his injury, Reich had lived in the darkness, and then at halftime of the Miami game came the dawn.

Ross benched the ineffective Gelbaugh in favor of Reich, and Reich delivered what would have sufficed for most anybody else as the game of his life.

"I hadn't heard that before, and it struck me," Reich said of his future wife's proverb. "She told me it before the Duke game when I was starting to feel better and it looked like I still wasn't going to play. But I decided to hang in there."

Reich completed 12 of 15 passes for 260 yards and three TDs as the Terps left the cocky Hurricanes speechless. He would go on to complete 64 percent of his passes that year, closing his college career by leading Maryland past Tennessee in the Sun Bowl.

When he arrived in Buffalo he impressed his coaches and teammates with his knowledge of the game, and when Kelly came aboard in Reich's second season, the two men who couldn't have had more polar opposite personalities worked more cohesively together than Fred Astaire and Ginger Rogers.

Kelly was the man on the field orchestrating the controlled chaos that was the no-huddle offense during Buffalo's Super Bowl years, but he readily admits he couldn't have done it without plenty of help, primarily from Reich.

"[Offensive coordinator] Ted Marchibroda was huge and another big part of it was Frank," said Kelly. "Having Frank there and being able to talk things over with Frank was so important for me. I remember many times Frank and I coming in before the meetings would start, the coaches would already have their game plan and we'd go up before the meetings and start drawing up plays on the chalkboard, things that we thought would work. It got to the point where Marchibroda would say, 'OK guys, show me what you've got.' Just for those guys to be able to have enough confidence in me to turn the offense over to me, that was huge."

Counting the playoffs, Reich made only 10 starts in his Bills career, and none was bigger than the wild-card playoff game against the Oilers, the same Oilers who one week earlier had blown out Buffalo in the 1992 regular-season finale at the Astrodome and knocked Kelly out of action with a knee injury.

THE GAME

January 3, 1993
BILLS 41, OILERS 38 (OT)

His is the name that is most commonly associated with the greatest comeback in NFL history. He was the miracle worker, the man who rallied the Bills against ridiculously long odds to pull out a game that seemed impossible when the scoreboard read 35-3 in favor of Houston two minutes into the third quarter.

But faster than those fans who had left Rich Stadium were trying to re-enter when they realized the Bills were making a game of it, Reich will tell you his role was no larger than anyone else's on the field that day.

"I didn't even throw for 300 yards in the game," he said. "It wasn't about any one individual. That's kind of what makes that game so special. That's always true in football—the tendency is to put the spotlight on one person. But unlike a golf tournament when you might come back from 10 shots behind on the last nine holes to win the Masters, this is a team game."

The Bills had won back-to-back AFC championships but had lost both Super Bowls to the Giants and Redskins. They were eager to make amends, but the Bills made the road to Super Bowl XXVII tough on themselves by losing three of their final five games.

That slump prevented them from capturing a fifth straight AFC East division title and relegated them to wild-card status as Miami won the division. This meant the Bills were not exempt from the first round of the playoffs, and Warren Moon's run-and-shoot Oilers were the designated opponent.

Making matters more difficult, the Bills would have to play the game without Kelly, who had suffered a knee injury in a 27-3 loss to Houston the week before.

The Bills had faith in Reich. In the six games he had started to that point in his career he had won four, and the only two losses came in the meaningless season finales of 1990 and 1991, when the Bills already had homefield advantage for the playoffs locked up and rested many starters.

That faith quite naturally was wavering at halftime when the Bills were booed into the locker room by the home fans that had watched in disbelief as Houston ran up a 28-3 lead.

And then two minutes into the third quarter when a Reich pass deflected off tight end Keith McKeller's hands and went right to cornerback Bubba McDowell who returned it 58 yards for a touchdown, Buffalo's plight seemed hopeless.

But Reich's faith—in himself, in his team, and of course in the Lord—never vacillated. Remember, he had already pulled off the comeback for the ages in college.

"Since I was part of a team in college that had a game like this, it wasn't like I had just read about it, I had experienced first-hand what it was like to be on a team and come back from 31 points and win a game," he said. "From that aspect, sure, I felt we could come back and win. But the driving thought was one play at a time, one series at a time, one touchdown at a time."

It all began on the series following McDowell's interception.

The Bills took possession at the 50 after Al Del Greco's squib kick caromed off Mark Maddox who then picked up the ball and returned it 15 yards. Ten plays later, Kenneth Davis—playing for Thurman Thomas who was knocked out of the game just before McDowell's interception with a hip pointer—plunged over from the one to make it 35-10.

Steve Christie then successfully recovered his own onside kick at the Buffalo 48, and 56 seconds later Reich lofted a 38-yard touchdown pass to Don Beebe. "The onside kick was a big momentum shift," said Reich. "That was definitely a turning point, but when you're down that much, the defense still had to make some big plays."

It did. The Oilers went three and out and a poor 25-yard Greg Montgomery punt gave the Bills the ball at their own 41. Four plays later Reich threaded a perfect strike to Reed over the middle for a 26-yard touchdown, and suddenly it was 35-24 with more than a quarter still left to play.

"When we scored to make it 35-24 late in the third quarter, that's when I thought it was really within reach," Reich said. "If the defense just kept playing the way they were playing and the offense kept executing, there was plenty of time."

Sure enough, the defense continued its startling about-face from the first-half flop as Henry Jones picked off a Moon pass and brought it back to the Houston 23. After two Davis runs for five yards and an incompletion, the Bills were faced with fourth-and-five. Following a timeout, coach Marv Levy eschewed the field goal, and the bold move paid off as Reich fired another laser to Reed in the end zone to make it 35-31.

"It wasn't what they were doing, it was what they weren't doing," Reich said. "You just lose a little bit of an edge. When I threw the interception that made it 35-3, you could sense it over on the other sideline—they're celebrating and they were thinking it was over. It's not like they quit playing, but they opened the door just a little bit. It was just a natural human instinct."

After an exchange of punts, Houston drove from its own 10 to the Buffalo 14. However, the Bills kept the Oilers out of the end zone and their hard work paid off when Montgomery—Houston's holder on placements—dropped the snap on a field goal attempt and the Bills took over at the 26. Within seven plays—one a 35-yard Davis run on third-and-four—Reich and Reed hooked up for the third straight possession, this time on a 17-yard score, and the Bills were ahead, 38-35, with 3:08 remaining.

"You can talk to all the players about this, but the thing that was evident was our players never quit," said Reed. "Not only the guys on the field, but the guys on the sideline. You talk about being in the zone. That was a team being in the zone."

The Oilers somehow regrouped and managed to force overtime when Moon—who completed a then NFL playoff-record 36 passes for a Houston playoff-record 371 yards—marched them 63 yards to set up Del Greco's tying 26-yard field goal with 12 seconds left.

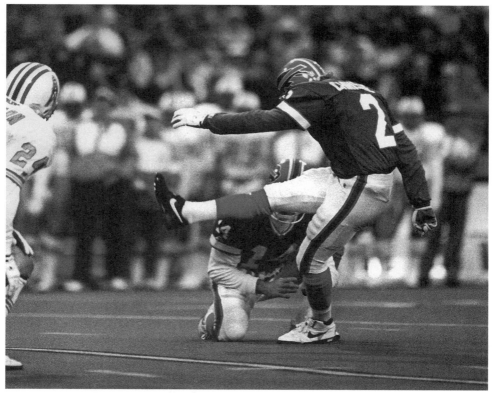

Steve Christie, out of Frank Reich's hold, kicks the game-winning field goal in overtime against the Oilers. **Courtesy of the Buffalo Bills**

Buffalo then lost the coin toss to start the extra period, but that wound up working in its favor because on the third play Nate Odomes intercepted a poorly thrown Moon pass and returned it to the Oilers 20. After two Davis plunges, Christie came on and kicked the game-winning 32-yard field goal to complete what Houston cornerback Cris Dishman termed not the greatest comeback in history, but the "biggest choke in history."

SINCE THE GAME

Reich played two more years in Buffalo before moving on to Carolina to become the expansion Panthers' first quarterback in 1995. His stint was brief, just three games before coach Dom Capers turned to rookie Kerry Collins.

Reich saw the most extensive playing time of his career in 1996 with the New York Jets when he took over for injured Neil O'Donnell and started seven games, setting single-season career highs for completions (175), attempts (331), yards (2,205) and touchdowns (15). He then spent his final two years with the Detroit Lions, again serving as a backup.

Upon retirement from football Reich enrolled in classes at the Reformed Theological Seminary in Charlotte, a nondenominational seminary founded in 1966 whose mission is to serve all forms of evangelical Christianity, particularly Presbyterian and Reformed.

He pursued a Master of Divinity degree with the intention of becoming either a pastor or a Christian public speaker. Ultimately he became director of the seminary.

As for the game against Houston, the game of his life, the game of the life of every true Bills fan, it is undoubtedly the proudest moment of his professional career, but only because it was so much more than just a football game.

"There's one aspect of the comeback, the victory and all the statistics of it, but the real value is how it transcends football and gives us strength and hope and confidence to live that kind of life in everything we do, not just on the football field," he said.

CHAPTER NINETEEN

Andre Reed

Position: Wide receiver
Number: 83
Years with Bills: 1985-99
Other teams: Redskins (2000)
College: Kutztown (Pennsylvania) State
Born: January 29, 1964
Hometown: Allentown, Pennsylvania
Current residence: San Diego, California
Current occupation: Broadcaster

Andre played in more games (221) than any player in Bills history…was named to the Pro Bowl seven times…his 87 touchdowns are tied for the team record with Thurman Thomas…all-time Bills leader in catches (941), receiving yards (13,095) and receiving TDs (86)…was inducted into the Division II college football hall of fame in 2002 and the Greater Buffalo Sports Hall of Fame in 2004.

THIS IS ANDRE REED

Andre Reed always knew what he wanted to do, but as a youngster growing up in Allentown, Pennsylvania, he had a tough time convincing his pals that he was going to someday play in the National Football League.

"Back when I was in school," Reed said, "I'd tell people I was going to play in the NFL and they'd say, 'Yeah Reed, sure, you're going to the NFL. What you're going to be doing is bagging groceries.'"

Tens of thousands of kids dream of playing a sport on a professional level, be it football, baseball, basketball or hockey. It's easy to dream it, easy to say it. It's not as easy to make it. In fact, the odds are astronomical, but Reed was one of the exceptions because he did everything that those boys who teased him—many of whom probably harbored similar dreams—failed to do: He worked harder than anyone to make his dream become reality.

Andre practiced with a fanatical purpose. He never turned off the blow-torch of desire that burned in his belly—whether for his Dieruff High School coach, Bruce Trotter; his two coaches at Kutztown State, George Baldwin and Al Leonzi; or the man who perhaps deserves the most credit for Reed's development as a player and a person—his father Calvin.

"I think I was born to play," Reed once said.

Calvin and Joyce Reed's four children—Andre, Tyrone, Dion, and sister Teshia—were all born to play. They were an athletically inclined brood and once Calvin saw the interest they had in sports, he made sure they put their talents to good use.

The boys played everything, but football was their passion, probably because it was Calvin's passion, and their introduction came in the midget league at the downtown Allentown youth center with their dad serving as coach. When they weren't involved with a team activity, they spent countless hours being put through the paces by their dad. He would take them to Fountain Park, or Valania Park or Roosevelt Park, and they would run laps and sprints, do calisthenics, run pass patterns against each other, and fine-tune their skills.

"We were the most competitive family in the City of Allentown," Andre said. "Everyone knew the Reeds. Whether we were playing in our yard or at the park, we always had some sort of game going."

Andre was a quarterback in his youth football days and later at Dieruff, but the skinny 130-pounder didn't become the starter in high school until his senior year after Rich Sniscak—now a high school head coach in Allentown—graduated.

Operating Trotter's veer offense, Andre led Dieruff to an undefeated season as he rushed for at least 100 yards on six occasions. Division I schools such as Penn State, Pittsburgh, West Virginia and Temple asked about

Andre Reed, the greatest receiver in Bills history, caught 941 passes for over 13,000 yards in his Buffalo career. **Courtesy of the Buffalo Bills**

Andre, but scholarship offers came with a stipulation: There would be no free ride unless Andre went to a junior college to accrue more experience and bulk up his frame, now up to 155 pounds, but still not strong enough to compete in big-time college football.

"They wanted me to go to a junior college, and I just didn't want to do it," he said. "I wasn't gung-ho about going to a junior college."

So he stayed close to home and chose to attend Kutztown, 20 miles outside Allentown. While playing for a Division II school generally means your football career ends as soon as your eligibility expires, Kutztown served as a launching pad thanks to a critical personnel decision. The coaching staff took one look at Reed, saw the quickness, the explosive athleticism, the tough-minded determination, and decided he'd be better off playing receiver rather than quarterback.

"They told me they could probably use me at wide receiver [as a freshman] if I wanted to play there," Reed recalled. "I was like, 'OK, um, sure, whatever you want.' I had never played wide receiver, but I adapted to the change pretty well. I guess that was a good move."

Never mind the long and winding road he was going to be traveling in Division II. Once he began catching passes instead of throwing them, his dream of playing in the NFL began to come into focus.

"There wasn't any doubt in my mind I could make it," he said. "Even though I didn't play at a big school I knew I could handle the competition. I knew if I got the chance to play, I could show my talents and show what I could do."

So did Elbert Dubenion. Dubenion had been a big-play receiver for the Bills throughout their AFL days in the 1960s and was then one of Buffalo's talent scouts. He caught a glimpse of Reed during his sophomore year, and his first instinct was to enroll him in the FBI's witness protection program so no other NFL scouts could find him.

"Ray Charles could see he was a great player," Dubenion said of Reed, who set nine school receiving records at Kutztown and was named to the Pennsylvania State Athletic Conference team three years in a row. "He was fast, caught the ball in traffic, he was just great. It didn't matter what level he came from, he could play."

Scouts from other teams did find Reed, but the Bills pulled their trigger in the fourth round in 1985 to draft him.

That was a miserable year in Buffalo, the second of back-to-back 2-14 seasons, but it was the year that Reed proved he belonged in the NFL and he remembers the exact moment when that realization hit him.

"It was in the first training camp, when we were actually in pads and hitting the first day," he said. "Vince Ferragamo threw me a pass, it was kind of high, and I jumped up and I think it was Don Wilson cut my legs out from under me. I came down hard but I still hung on to the ball, got up and went back to the huddle and I said to myself, 'If this is what the NFL is about, I think I just passed my first test.'"

Fifteen years later when he was released in a salary cap move, Reed had passed every other test. He exited Buffalo having played more games in a Buffalo uniform (221) than anyone in team history, and his team receiving marks of 941 catches, 13,095 yards and 87 touchdowns may never be surpassed.

GAME DAY SETTING

Monday Night Football—a national stage—and the four-time defending AFC champion Bills were getting the crap kicked out of them by the Pittsburgh Steelers.

During the Hall of Fame career of quarterback Jim Kelly there were many wonderful triumphs but also a few horrifying defeats, and this 23-10 loss to the Steelers in 1994 at Three Rivers Stadium with an entire football nation watching was one of the worst.

It was a disaster for the Bills—Kelly in particular—and he took out his frustration on his longtime battery mate, Reed. On a play where Kelly was lambasted by Rod Woodson, fumbling the ball away to Pittsburgh defensive lineman Gerald Williams for a touchdown, Kelly faulted Reed. He missed a

Kelly audible at the line of scrimmage and did not run the proper hot route that would have allowed Kelly to get rid of the ball, possibly for a positive gain. Instead, Kelly paid the painful price, then came to the sideline and chewed out Reed.

Never one to back down, Reed returned Kelly's vitriol with equal vehemence, and wouldn't you know it, those omnipresent *Monday Night Football* cameras caught the entire two-way verbal tirade.

On the October night in 2004 when Reed was inducted into the Greater Buffalo Sports Hall of Fame and Kelly was there to share in the celebration, Kelly remembered that night in Pittsburgh and succinctly put it into perspective.

"When you have a duo like me and Andre who played together for so long, you're going to have your times when you have good days and bad days," Kelly said. "The thing about Andre is he just wanted to be the best, the top guy all the time. I knew he was my go-to guy, I knew where my bread was buttered, but there were times when he knew he wasn't going to get the ball and he'd take a play or two off. And I was one who didn't want anybody taking a play off."

On that play in Pittsburgh, it was Kelly's interpretation that Reed had taken the play off. Reed disagreed. They argued, and everyone sitting in their living rooms watching the game saw it unfold up close and personal. What they didn't see was about a minute later, the two players coming together right there on the sideline and apologizing to each other.

"Everything wasn't going to be peachy keen," Reed said of his relationship with Kelly. "In order for us to be as good as we were, we had to have arguments, too. It was all part of the game, and it was definitely part of that game."

When Kelly joined the team a year after Reed, a franchise revival began. Right away, the two Pennsylvania boys clicked because Kelly knew he needed Reed, and Reed knew he needed Kelly.

What a pair they made. During the 11 years they played catch with each other, ending in 1996 when Kelly retired, Kelly threw 67 touchdown passes to Reed, at the time the third highest total for a quarterback/receiver combo in NFL history. Of the 41 times Reed surpassed 100 yards receiving in a regular-season game, Kelly was the quarterback 29 times.

"When it came down to Sunday at one o'clock, I believed in him and he believed in me, and we were all out there for the same reason, to win," said Reed. "That's what it was all about. The only way I got better is if he got better and vice-versa. We were one of the greatest combinations ever, let's face it."

THE GAME

November 20, 1994
BILLS 29, PACKERS 20

In the summer of 2002, Kelly and a bunch of his old Bills teammates reunited for a charity flag football game at the University at Buffalo that benefited Kelly's charity, Hunter's Hope, founded in honor of his son Hunter who suffers from Krabbe Disease.

Kelly and the Bills took on a team of former NFL stars led by his old AFC East rival from Miami, Dan Marino, and while the game was all in the name of fun, make no mistake: Kelly and the Bills wanted to win.

How much?

"Andre's favorite saying when he broke the huddle was, 'Right here, right here, Jim,' meaning throw the ball to him," Kelly recalled. "We did the flag football game over at UB a few years ago, and we break the huddle and Andre's saying, 'Right here, Jim, right here.' Don Beebe's in the huddle laughing and he says, 'Some things just never change.' That's why Andre was so good. He always wanted to be the best."

Reed was never better than on an unusually mild late November day at Rich Stadium in 1994, a day that he repeated, "Right here, Jim, right here," over and over and Kelly dutifully and wisely answered, "OK, Andre, OK."

Against a Green Bay team that was on the verge of becoming a Super Bowl champion but wasn't quite there yet, Reed played the game of his life as he caught 15 passes for 191 yards—both career highs—and two touchdowns during Buffalo's 29-20 victory over the Packers. At the time the 15 receptions were the fourth highest single-game total in NFL history, and it remains the Bills' team record.

"I was in the zone that game," Reed said. "If there was such a thing as a zone, guys like [Michael] Jordan and Tiger [Woods] and all those guys talk about it, that was a game when I was in the zone. Every player tries to get into the zone, but when a player actually gets there, it's like a bubble and no one else can get into it and you feel like you're invincible. I can talk about other games, but that game I felt invincible."

And what made it so special is that it came six days after the commotion in Pittsburgh, and it at least momentarily quieted the fans in Buffalo who were in an uproar over the fact that their Bills were in danger of missing the playoffs for the first time in seven years.

"That Monday night game in Pittsburgh, it was one of those games where things didn't go right and they thought Jim and I were bickering about this and bickering about that," said Reed. "And really it was just our way of trying to find each other at that time and to get back on track. We came back the next week, and I caught 15 balls for almost 200 yards, which dispelled all the myths about what supposedly happened the game before."

Clearly anxious to wash away the bitter memories of Pittsburgh, the Buffalo offense drove to touchdowns on its first two possessions for a 14-0 lead. Kelly began playing pitch and catch with Reed on the first series, completing a 15-yard pass that helped lead to Thurman Thomas's five-yard scoring run.

After a Green Bay punt, the Bills started their next drive at their 20 and, faced with a second-and-18, Kelly fired a 19-yard completion to Reed. Later there was a seven-yard pass to Reed, and then on third-and-five from the Packers' 15, Reed ran a crossing route over the middle—his specialty throughout his career—and Kelly hit him in stride for a touchdown.

"I know I was going against Terrell Buckley a lot," Reed said of the cocky, risk-taking Green Bay cornerback. "He was a young corner at the time, his task was to stop me, and it was just my day. Jim was going to me and it felt good. It was man to man a lot, and I caught a lot of this and I caught a lot of that. I made some catches over people. It was just one of those games, like no other."

When the Bills made it 17-0 in the second quarter, Reed kept the drive alive by drawing a pass interference penalty on Buckley. He also beat Buckley for a 28-yard gain down the right sideline, and he caught a six-yard pass with Buckley in one-on-one coverage.

Later in the quarter Brett Favre was intercepted by Buffalo cornerback Mickey Washington, and two plays after his 36-yard return to the Green Bay 13, Reed ran another route over the middle and Kelly found him for the score and a 24-0 cushion.

Favre's 29-yard touchdown pass to Sterling Sharpe 1:03 before halftime awakened the Packers, but Kelly's answer to that was a 35-yard pass to Russell Copeland and his eighth hookup of the half with Reed, a four-yarder that positioned Steve Christie for a final-play 51-yard field goal.

As the Bills left the field ahead, 27-6, the crowd gave them a standing ovation. Pittsburgh was definitely a thing of the past.

The second half wasn't nearly as much fun for Buffalo as Favre rallied his team to within 27-20 with a pair of third-quarter touchdown passes, but Kelly and Reed went back to work on one of the key possessions of the day in the fourth. Needing to kill some clock to keep the ball away from Favre, the Bills churned out four first downs and Reed made three more receptions for 42 yards. Buffalo chewed up nearly seven minutes, and the victory was later cemented when the defense recorded a safety in the final minutes.

When it came time to award game balls in the locker room, Kelly simply repeated what he had been doing all day. He tossed a spiral to Reed. Reed then did what he had been doing all day. He caught it.

"We need to argue a little more," Reed joked as the room filled with laughter.

SINCE THE GAME

Kelly played through 1996 before calling it quits, and Reed soldiered on for four more years in Buffalo and a last season in Washington following his release by the Bills. He returned to Buffalo in September 2001 and signed a one-day contract so he could officially retire as a Bill.

Reed and his wife, Cyndi, and their two children, Auburn and Andre, lived in Orlando for a couple years and Reed ran a fitness spa. Now the family lives in San Diego and Reed works as a broadcaster. He was an analyst on Fox Sports' coverage of NFL Europe, and he does work for Fox Sports Net on the San Diego Chargers' pre- and postgame shows.

Jim Kelly and Andre Reed share some love after one of the 67 touchdowns they combined on during their days in Buffalo. **Courtesy of the Buffalo Bills**

His numbers would suggest he should be a shoo-in for induction in the Pro Football Hall of Fame. However, in an era when passing is prevalent, numbers don't mean as much as they once did, and there is speculation that without a Super Bowl ring on his finger, Reed may not be able to follow Kelly and Levy into the Canton shrine.

"At this point, if it's going to happen, it's going to happen, it's not in my control," he said. "The only thing I can control is what I did on the field, and I thought I did what was necessary to be successful. If it does happen, that would just be the culmination of a lot of hard work and preparation and dedication. That's what the Hall of Fame's about. It's about being prepared every year and going out there and playing your best and have an opportunity. Buffalo gave me that opportunity."

CHAPTER TWENTY

Eric Moulds

Position: Wide receiver
Number: 80
Years with Bills: 1996-present
Other teams: None
Born: July 17, 1973
College: Mississippi State
Hometown: Lucedale, Mississippi
Current residence: Orchard Park, New York
Current occupation: Active player

Eric was the Bills' first-round draft choice (No. 24 overall) in 1996…holds Bills' single-season records for receptions (100 in 2002) and receiving yards (1,368 in 1998)…trails only Andre Reed on Bills' career list for receptions, receiving yards and receiving touchdowns…started the 2005 season with a team-record streak of having caught at least one pass in 110 straight games.

THIS IS ERIC MOULDS

It didn't come as a surprise to anyone who knows him that a couple of years ago Eric Moulds, by then an established All-Pro wide receiver for the Bills, was contemplating putting his dazzling football career on hold to take a stab at pro basketball.

After all, a decade earlier he had put his dazzling basketball career on hold to pursue football.

"I enjoy being here and playing in the NFL," Moulds said when word of his possible decision leaked out in January of 2002, "but basketball was my first love, and it's something I always wondered what might have been."

From the time he was old enough to walk, Moulds could be found in the yard of his divorced mother's home in the tiny town of Lucedale, Mississippi perfecting his dribbling and shooting skills, pretending he was Magic Johnson or Julius Erving and dreaming about taking it to the hoop in NBA arenas around the country.

He played in the morning, he played in the afternoon, and he played in the evening. He played alone, he played with friends, and he played with his mother, Mae, if she had time between working the day shift in a nursing home and the night shift as a nurse at the local hospital.

And wow, he could play. By the time Moulds advanced to George County High School he was already one of the best players in Mississippi, and by his junior year he had college recruiters from most of the big-time Division I programs, including Duke and Kentucky, knocking at his door.

There was no doubt that Moulds was going to be attending college, and he wasn't going to have to pay for it. However, along about his junior year the question no longer became, "Which school was going to pay the freight?" It became, "In which sport is Moulds going to accept a scholarship?"

Moulds had never shown an interest in football until the end of his sophomore year at George County, but he thought he'd give the sport a try when he became a junior. He showed up for spring practice and blew the coaches away with his athleticism, and right then football coach Hal Holmes knew the young man was going to have to make a career choice.

"The first day that I actually saw him run some routes and catch the football just in shorts, I thought that he might play on Sunday," said Holmes. "In high school Eric was six foot two, 185, and could run a 4.4 in the 40. He had no football experience, but he was such a man among boys in a lot of areas."

Moulds was the team's leading receiver and he returned four punts for touchdowns in the first five games of his inaugural football season. Then as a senior he led the Rebels to an 8-2 record and capped his abbreviated high

After a couple years, Eric Moulds finally established himself in Buffalo—he's on his way to becoming one of the team's all-time greats. **Courtesy of the Buffalo Bills**

school gridiron career with a game that Holmes maintains is the greatest he has ever seen by a high schooler.

Now another batch of college recruiters came flocking to Lucedale, this group intent on convincing Moulds to play football for them, and to the surprise of many in his hometown, though not Holmes, Moulds listened.

During his senior basketball season he averaged 30 points per game, earned his third all-state honor, and received a phone call from Duke coach Mike Krzyzewski who was about to win his second consecutive national championship in the spring of 1992. Krzyzewski asked Moulds to join the powerhouse Blue Devils in their annual quest for college basketball supremacy, but Moulds told Coach K, "Thanks, but no thanks," and opted to play football at nearby Mississippi State for coach Jackie Sherrill.

Moulds was forced to sit out his first year in order to become academically eligible, then improved every year and when he left Starkville he ranked third all-time in catches (118) and receiving yards (2,022) and with a school-record 17 touchdowns.

The Bills selected him with the 24th overall pick in the first round of the 1996 draft. Nine years later he ranks second behind Andre Reed in all the major career receiving categories, and if he stays with Buffalo and remains healthy, he has a chance to surpass all of Reed's Hall of Fame-worthy numbers.

Who knows what would have become of Moulds had he stuck with basketball. "Some guys think I could have played in the NBA and had a big impact," he said.

Well, if it's an impact that he was looking to make, he has made one in the NFL, and he knows it. "I have no regrets. I think I made the right choice."

GAME DAY SETTING

Two years into his NFL career, the Bills and their fans weren't wondering whether Moulds had an 'A' game, they were wondering if he had 'any' game.

"It was difficult because of the situation I was in," said Moulds, who caught only 49 passes those first two years and was unable to supplant either Andre Reed or Quinn Early from Marv Levy's starting lineup.

"I was behind Quinn and Andre and we used two-tight end sets a lot, so it limited me from being on the field. I just had to adjust to that and it was difficult, because coming from college, a first-round pick and with that pressure, I had to deal with that."

When the 1997 season ended and Moulds returned home to Lucedale, he didn't need his mother to tell him that he hadn't had a very good year, though she did anyway. Teammate Thurman Thomas told him.

As the players were cleaning out their lockers following the Bills' disappointing 6-10 season, Thomas sidled over to Moulds's stall, sat down and told him, "You're going into your third year. It's about time you turn your life around and start doing what it takes to play in this league."

Moulds knew he hadn't played well and he was well aware that he was being perceived as a first-round bust. His receiving numbers were paltry, and after setting a team record with 1,205 kickoff return yards as a rookie in 1996, his production had dwindled dramatically in that area as well in 1997.

Away from football, Moulds's life had become a soap opera. He had fathered four children out of wedlock, he was accused of not paying child support for his oldest child, and he pled guilty to two charges of second-degree harassment of two college women.

In the winter months of 1998, Moulds began a grueling conditioning program—with the help of NFL star cornerbacks Deion Sanders and Aeneas Williams—designed to shave 15 unnecessary pounds and turn the pounds that were left into chiseled muscle.

"The way I grew up and the way I was taught, you never give up, it's never over until it's over," said Moulds. "That was the main thing I was thinking in that off season. I tried to work hard and I thought about the things that happened during the season and I tried to improve on the things that I wasn't that good at. My mom could tell I was starting to mature, so she said, 'I think this is going to be your year.'"

Mother always knows best.

Wade Phillips, who had taken over as Buffalo's coach for the retired Levy, named Moulds a 1998 starter, and when new starting quarterback Rob Johnson went down with a rib injury in the fifth game, backup Doug Flutie took over, and he and Moulds became one of the most dynamic duos in the league.

By year's end, he had set a new Bills record for receiving yards in a season with 1,368. That total, and his 20.4 average per catch, ranked second in the league, and his achievements were a huge reason why the 10-6 Bills made it back to the playoffs as a wild-card team after a one-year hiatus, destination Miami where Moulds was ready to rewrite the NFL record book.

THE GAME

January 2, 1999
DOLPHINS 24, BILLS 17

During the 1998 season, Miami cornerbacks Sam Madison and Terrell Buckley became the most lethal tandem in the NFL.

Miami's defense ranked No. 1 in points allowed (265), No. 3 in yards allowed, and with Madison and Buckley leading the way with eight interceptions apiece, just one behind league-leader Ty Law of New England, the Dolphins picked off a league-leading 29 passes, the fourth highest team total in the NFL during the 1990s.

Why were they so successful? Doug Flutie espoused an inflammatory theory in the week leading up to Buffalo's playoff showdown against the archrival Dolphins.

"It will be important for the officials to pull their flags if they start tugging and pulling as usual," Flutie said in reference to Madison's and Buckley's aggressive, physical style of play. "That's something that they do and they walk that fine line and get away with it. They usually get one or two penalties at the most and the rest of the game they push the envelope a little bit."

When Flutie's words filtered down to South Florida, Buckley and Madison erupted.

"That really ticks me off for him to say something like that," said Madison. "They have to get him out of the pocket because he's too short to see over the defensive line. We're going to be ready for that and we're going to get him on the ground and shove some Flutie Flakes down his throat. That motivates me, and their receivers are going to have to be ready to play Saturday."

Game on. Moulds was more than ready for the challenge.

Although the Bills lost the game in heartbreaking fashion, Moulds played the game of his life as he caught nine passes for an NFL playoff-record 240 yards.

"There was a lot of hype before that game because guys were talking back and forth," said Moulds. "But we thought we had a great chance to win that game. Jimmy Johnson was their coach so we knew we'd have opportunities in man to man to be able to go downfield and make some plays that way."

Moulds did all he could do, and when it was over, Miami linebacker Zach Thomas was left shaking his head and saying, "That guy's unbelievable."

Unbelievable would be an appropriate way to describe the first play from scrimmage that sultry Saturday afternoon, a play that served as a microcosm of Moulds's day—magnificent yet unfulfilling.

Moulds beat Buckley's press coverage at the line and sprinted downfield, Flutie fired a perfect pass, Moulds made the grab and seemed headed for a jaw-dropping touchdown. Instead, Buckley caught him from behind and punched the ball out and safety Brock Marion recovered for the Dolphins. It was a 65-yard gain, but it was all for naught.

"It was a situation when the coaches wanted an opportunity to go up the field just to let them know that we were going to try to make some big plays," said Moulds. "I caught the ball and I looked back and I couldn't see him, then I looked back a second time and he made a great play to knock the ball out."

Miami turned around and marched 57 yards to a 31-yard Olindo Mare field goal, then made it 6-0 when Mare capped the Dolphins' second possession with a 40-yard field goal. Here the game took an odd twist. Johnson called for a surprise onside kick, but the alert Bills foiled the gamble as Dan Brandenburg recovered. On first down Moulds beat Buckley again, this time for a 37-yard gain to the Miami five, and two plays later the Bills were ahead when Thurman Thomas plunged up the middle for a one-yard touchdown.

In the third quarter the teams exchanged turnovers, then punts before Dan Marino directed a 52-yard drive that ended with Karim Abdul-Jabbar's three-yard TD run. Stanley Pritchett's two-point conversion run made it 14-7 and the sellout crowd was back into the game. Less than two minutes later, they were silent again thanks to Moulds.

Moulds drew a 29-yard interference penalty on Dolphins cornerback Patrick Surtain, caught a 23-yard pass to move the ball to the Miami 32, and then beat cornerback Jerrel Wilson one on one for a 32-yard TD reception. Tie game.

"It was a blitz call and I was in the slot and I knew that we had a chance to go deep if they blitzed," said Moulds. "They showed that on film and I was reading that linebacker. I know Flutie saw it because he gave me a peak when he looked at the linebacker. I just ran a streak route, and he hit me in stride, and I made the play. I carried somebody into the end zone, one of those situations where I knew I had a chance to score the touchdown but I shrugged off a tackle."

Unfazed, Miami opened a 10-point lead in the fourth quarter, setting the stage for a wild finish. Thanks to a 31-yard reception by Moulds and a 22-yard interference penalty on Buckley drawn by Moulds, the Bills were in scoring position at the Miami 10 as the game was stopped for the two-minute warning. On the next play, Andre Reed caught a pass over the middle and was ruled down inches short of the goal line. Thinking he had scored, he jumped up quickly and bumped into field judge Steve Zimmer, drawing a 15-yard penalty and an automatic ejection from the game.

"I feel like we got robbed," remembered Moulds. "I ran a slant on the back side and Andre had a play where he came in on a shallow route and we were going to dump it real quick and let him make a play. From my vantage point it looked like he was in. The referee on my side was looking and I said, 'He's in,' but it wasn't his call, it was the guy on the other side who called it and he said he was on the one-yard line. Then Andre jumped up and bumped the official and they moved us back and took away our momentum."

The Bills wound up settling for a Steve Christie field goal, then recovered their second onside kick of the day, this one by Kurt Schulz at the Buffalo 31 with 1:30 left to play. However, thanks to the unfortunate Reed ruling, the Bills needed a touchdown to tie.

They got within five yards before the Dolphins turned them away.

Continuing his amazing day, Moulds made a 30-yard grab on the first snap that allowed him to break ex-Viking Cris Carter's playoff record of 227 receiving yards set against San Francisco in 1987. The Bills went on to convert three third downs, including a five-yard catch by Moulds, before Flutie took his last timeout with 17 seconds remaining.

The play call was for a slant over the middle, but Flutie never had a chance to throw it as Trace Armstrong hammered him and forced a fumble that Shane Burton recovered to preserve Miami's first postseason victory over the Bills in four tries.

In the blink of an eye, the Bills' season was over, and it left a sour taste in Moulds's mouth.

Eric Moulds has played in just three playoff games, but in this one against Miami in 1999 he set the all-time postseason record for receiving yards in a game at 240.
Courtesy of the Buffalo Bills

"It was frustrating because just like the Tennessee game [a year later, the infamous Music City Miracle loss], we knew that if we won that Miami game we had a chance to go to the Super Bowl," said Moulds.

SINCE THE GAME

In the five seasons since, the Bills have failed to make it back to the post-season, through no fault of Moulds.

In 2000 he nearly surpassed his receiving yardage record set in 1998 with 1,326 yards on a career-best and team-record 94 catches, and then in 2002 he became the first Bill in history to reach 100 receptions in a season as he earned his third Pro Bowl invitation.

Through the 2004 campaign, Moulds had 594 catches for 8,162 yards and 45 touchdowns as he continues his pursuit of Reed's team career records.

The individual achievements do not drive Moulds, though. He cares only about winning, and Buffalo's prolonged absence from the postseason weighs a little heavier with each passing season.

"It stinks," said Moulds, the last holdover from the Marv Levy era. "Any time you look at an organization like this that has been to four straight Super Bowls, you're used to being in the playoffs and the fans getting excited about getting their tickets to the Super Bowl. Right now, we don't have that type of fanfare."

Celebrate the Heroes of New York Sports
in These Other Releases from Sports Publishing!

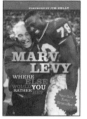

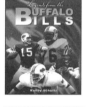